FINANCIAL
DETOX

16 SECRETS TO DETOX YOUR FINANCES
AND ACHIEVE FINANCIAL FREEDOM

FERNANDO PALACIO
CATALINA CORTÉS

FINANCIAL DETOX

16 SECRETS TO DETOX YOUR FINANCES AND ACHIEVE FINANCIAL FREEDOM

Fernando Palacio
Catalina Cortés

Editorial PSL

Acknowledgements

So much and so many to give thanks to. In our journey as business owners and investors, we have had incredible mentors who have inspired us with their example and advised us with their wisdom and financial intelligence.

María Mercedes, an example of attitude, responsibility and dynamism, the best possible mother.

Our first mentors, Mario and Betty Orsini, taught us a lot about business, but above all about life. We have also had the influence of wonderful people, such as Carlos Eduardo Castellanos, Claudia Santos and Camilo Pinto, with whom we have learned on the battlefield.

On a financial intelligence level specifically, we thank the wonderful authors who preceded us, and on a more personal level Vladimir Pándura, a star in the matter, who has advised us wisely.

THANK YOU, THANK YOU, THANK YOU

CONTENTS

Title Page   3

Copyright   4

Dedication   5

Introduction   9

Part one   19

Cashflow, Cashflow, Cashflow.   21

Is it worth saving today?   29

Compound interest and why you can dream big   39

Is saving possible? Hack your Biology   49

@Coach_financiero, what do i do? ¿pay off debts or start   61
saving?

#Stop_financial_bullying   67

Part two   75

Lower expenses: the magic of creating a positive cashflow 77
now!

Debt restructuring, refinance under your own terms.   89

Monetize what you consume   99

Sharing economy   109

Freedom cashflow: detox from bad debts   113

Part three   125

It's time to…increase your income!   127

Low-cost venture – create your own money making machine   139

Today's network marketing: monetize your social media   145

Low cost real estate investments   159

Info-entrepreneurship:monetize your knowledge   171

Conclusion   177

Assembling the puzzle   179

About The Author   185

INTRODUCTION

"Success is a lousy teacher. It seduces smart people into thinking they can't lose." - Bill Gates

There is enormous ignorance about how most of the world's forunes are created. Many believe that it is a matter of inheritance or a stroke of luck. Others believe that only those who have a special talent or "gift" can achieve it.

There is nothing further from reality. Most fortunes are created in a single lifetime, starting with very little, with nothing, or even in negative (with debt). Today we have an incredible example of this because the largest companies in the world, the most attractive, the fastest growing, didn't even exist 5, 10 or 15 years ago. Companies such as Google, Airbnb, Uber, Rappi, Glovo, Facebook, Amazon and Instagram, are very recent and show us that it's possible to start and create empires from nothing and in a short period of time. Many of these were started by young people from their bedroom or garage, with almost no investment.

In modern culture, on the other hand, there is a perception that being rich implies "a great transaction" or "a great opportunity" that, legal or not, will lead to financial success. Unfortunately, the disastrous legacy of drug trafficking and the culture of "reality shows" has contributed to the strengthening of the collective belief that someone, one day, could "discover me" and then I'll become rich, successful and happy or even worse, that the rich are rich because they did something illegal.

This way of thinking causes a lot of damage, because instead of working on their personal skills and development as human beings, many people sit and wait for something external and fortuitous to change their lives. It's sad to see how some even think that what will change their lives may be the government or a political party. This way they renounce to their power and become victims of their environment.

We could say that humanity suffers from an intoxication of incorrect and harmful financial information. I once heard that what hurts us the most isn't what we don't know, but what we know and isn't true. That is why it's essential to do a mental detox of all this false information and in turn replace these lies with new ideas that will help you attract money and think in a way that is consistent with your financial goals. It is logical to feel enormous frustration when you want to achieve certain results and at the same time you harbor destructive beliefs and practices that go against those wishes. From this contradiction derives the name of this book: **FINANCIAL DETOX**. Throughout these pages, we intend to help you identify negative ideas that inhabit you and almost everyone, and that have been the cause of most of their financial problems. Together we are going to walk a path of detoxifying our minds from all that mental weeds that have been instilled in us and we are going to plant new seeds that will bring fruits of economic prosperity, freedom and unlimited possibilities.

After more than 25 years in the world of entrepreneurship and investment, we can say that there is nothing further from reality than that set of negative ideas about finance. Wealth is built day by day. First, working on yourself, becoming good at what you do, having clarity about what you want in life and dedicating your time to improve yourself as an individual in the necessary areas that will lead you to be that person who has that life that you long for. Parallel to this, it is vital that you develop financial intelligence so that you learn how to save and invest your money. Saving and investing will be the accelerator that will allow your efforts to be the gasoline of a rocket aimed at wealth and that, once you achieve your success, you keep it.

Achieving financial wealth and executing a foolproof plan requires decision making and determination. This plan will require consistency, discipline, and emotional intelligence. Above all, it will require a change in values. A value is nothing more than a concept or an idea to which we assign certain value. It can be freedom, courage, security, family, etc. The set of values that we give priority to are those that shape our life. For example, it is common for many employees to not start a business because in their lives the value of "security" prevails. Prioritizing "security" as a value can reach the point of ignoring the reality that today, being an employee may be less safe than being an entrepreneur. However, if we grew up like most, in an environment in which our parents and teachers repeated to us in one way or another the message that "employment is safe" or "get a steady, secure job", this belief remains installed in our subconscious mind and if we don't do something to change it, it'll be almost impossible for us to have the courage to start a business and conquer a different life.

What we have learned, observed, and verified in our own lives is that the key to becoming rich is to create a positive cash-flow every month, which is accomplished in a very simple way: earning more than what you spend, or what is the same, with a different meaning: spending less than what you earn! The first meaning is focused on increasing your income and the other on reducing your expenses. Depending on your current financial situation, one of these two approaches will be more relevant. For example, if you have a good income that comes from different sources, but uncontrollable expenses that don't allow you to see where your money is going and why you cannot save and invest, the focus should be on *spending less than what you earn*; that is, reduce, refinance, restructure and control your expenses, which are nothing more than those cracks through which your money escapes every month. On the contrary, if you already live tight with expenses and lowering them even further would substantially decrease your quality of life; your approach should be on *earning more than what you spend*, with a focus on increasing your income and diversifying it. In any case, our experience is that most people need to do both, learn to control their expenses, adjusted to a budget and at the same time, increase their income in quantity, but above all in quality. You will learn all this in this book.

When you have a positive cashflow, you have a wonderful problem to solve: What do I do with the extra money that I have left each month? This will surely be an invitation to enter the world of investments, which will allow you to have a vision of a prosperous and unlimited future.

On the contrary, if your expenses exceed your income, you will live in a state of poverty and it'll be very difficult for you to believe that a different and abundant future awaits you. You won't find any sense in establishing a wealth plan because you will have nothing to feed it with, and your hopes will be tied up to something as utopian as winning the lottery or having access to an inheritance from an unknown wealthy relative.

NO CASHFLOW TODAY = NO RICH FUTURE
Is this clear enough?

In January 1998, I attended a large business event in Tampa, USA. As I entered the stadium, a hockey arena with around 25,000 people, the group of colleagues with whom I attended, observed a Japanese man at the gates of the event, handing out a series of purple cassettes for free. He had a booth that didn't say much and we looked at him like an insurance salesman or something like that, desperate to make sales. Most of the people who passed by him completely ignored him and even tried to avoid him, diverting their way. Around 11pm they called the next speaker to the stage and it turned out to be the Hawaiian-Japanese man that we had all wanted to avoid; his name: Robert Kiyosaki. After hearing him talk about the rat race, the cashflow quadrant, and advice from his Rich Dad vs. his Poor Dad (which would become one of the greatest personal finance bestsellers of all time), we were all absolutely ecstatic! We ran to the booth that we had seen when entering the event, to realize that there was nothing left. It looked as if it had been looted by vandals!

The unknown man, for us and for the majority of the planet at that time, became one of the modern gurus of economy, who predicted the crisis of 2008, which nobody saw coming, and is currently an eminence in the world of entrepreneurship and investments.

From that day on, I dedicated myself to studying his work, reading and listening to all the material he put out for sale. I didn't care if it was about entrepreneurship, business thinking, financial investments, real estate, sales, gold ... I've been a very good student of all the material that Robert Kiyosaki has produced and I am proud to say that I didn't just study it, but have applied it with discipline.

A couple of years later I met my wife Cata and although at first we had disagreements regarding money management, I must say that once she understood the principles that Kiyosaki teaches and began to change her mindset towards a business and investment mentality, she became the best business partner I could imagine. On social media you will find us on Facebook as **Fer and Cata Palacio**, **@ferycatapalacio on Instagram**, as well as our **@coach_financiero (financial coach)** account on Instagram or **Coach_Financiero Global on Facebook**. In the workshops we offer, if we are fortunate enough to get to know each other, we are simply Fer and Cata, as we will also refer to each other in this book, since we want to make you feel as if we were in your living room or drinking coffee, while we share what we have learned and our experiences with you.

In this book we're going to share with you a complete system so that, no matter where you are, you become rich. We'll start with different keys and ways to increase your monthly cashflow. That is, we are going to make practical recommendations that you can apply immediately to increase your income and reduce your expenses. We will teach you how, with that increase in monthly cashflow, you can create a Wave. This wave will begin by cleaning up your past financial mistakes, eliminating your bad debts; it will continue by filling a safety pond so you can start saving and investing, and when that wave picks up, it will turn into a tsunami that will carry you into financial freedom and wealth. Then the life you've always dreamt of will be an imminent possibility.

We want to clarify, that for us wealth is not represented by a figure accumulated in a bank or investment account. Our goal was never to accumulate capital. The definition of wealth may be different for each person and for us it means being able to live the life we want, without any limitation, having the assets and investments that provide us with that lifestyle, without having to work for money and still continue living with a percentage of what we earn, so that we continue investing and growing our personal finances. In other words, for us being rich is having an experience of life without limits and in permanent expansion.

In order to transmit to you how to achieve all this, we will base ourselves on the application of our own principles of financial intelligence, which we have been learning for more than 20 years, from the hands of the world's leading business and financial teachers. I say "we have been learning" because we continue to learn and I want you to know that we have applied and verified what we share here, because we don't like to teach something that we haven't corroborated.

Applying the principles that we will share in this book allowed us to achieve our financial freedom early in life; we generate cashflow with our businesses and investments in an amount greater than what we spend, without having to work for anyone, and we achieved it before the age of 30. We thrived before the age of 40, having built a portfolio of assets, between businesses and investments, that produced us a large cashflow of money with which we could live in the best properties, drive the best cars and travel the world, while continuing to build our businesses and investments. Today we live a life without limits, in which we continue to grow and expand. In addition, we can dedicate ourselves to what we love to do: share principles of financial intelligence, start up new proyects, give conferences around the world and have time to enjoy as a couple.

We currently live between Barcelona, Spain, because it is the city in the world that we like the most and Bogotá, Colombia, our beloved home country. There have been times when we have spent a third part of the year in Bogotá, another in Barcelona and another traveling the world, staying in the best hotels and enjoying the best tourism. We don't feel tied down to any place and we can design each day as we want, and that often means staying at home or walking our dog, without any rush. We share this with you, without the intention of wanting to be more or better than anyone else, neither to flaunt or show off; We do it because we know that anyone who, with dedication and commitment, applies the principles of financial intelligence that we will teach in this book and becomes an active and eternal student of financial intelligence, can build what we have built and without a doubt, much, much more. We share all of this with you because we want you to, no matter where you are right now, have faith that you can change your future and you can start today.

Also, we want to tell you that we have failed many times in businesses and investments and we have lost a lot of money;

businesses that seemed infallible, with perfect associates and the necessary capital, and have gone bankrupt at the speed of light. We have made investments that were sold to us as "100% safe" and have failed. There have been times where we have felt like we've lost everything and have had to start over, not exactly from scratch, but with a negative balance of hundreds of thousands of dollars, after liquidating everything. If you have lost and have fallen, we want to tell you that in those "failures" lies your greatest treasure. Not much is learned on the peak of mountains of success. Many times victories build up our ego and prevent us from seeing the lessons. On the contrary, in the defeats, in the falls and in the valleys of life, where we feel stagnant and it seems that nothing is happening, is where the true teaching happens. If we are able to free ourselves from self-pity and guilt, it is in those falls that we grow, it is there that we become better and more resistant. That is also our case; it was in the falls when we learned the greatest treasures and teachings of our life. In addition, let us bear in mind that every time we climb to the top of a mountain, we can only go down from there, to then go back up again. With time, we learned not to ask for a life without problems or valleys, instead ask for the wisdom to learn in those falls and valleys and harvest the fruits of the seeds of learning in hard times. In most cases, these fruits manifest as improvements in yourself, in your abilities, in your quality as a human being and in your level of consciousness. So, dear reader, if you are down, have had falls or have been in valleys in your life, don't worry, rather occupy yourself in learning the lesson that that situation has come to teach you. Understand how that valley presents itself to show you what you don't want in your life and to give you one of the two most important keys to success: clarity. When you have clarity of what you want in your life, you're already on 50% of the way, and the best way to obtain it is almost always by being clear about what you don't want. The other fundamental key to success is energy, which is derived from passion and love for what you do. On another occasion we will talk more about how, when these two keys come together in life, we're able to build anything.

We have been fortunate to have teachers and to build relationships with amazing people who have become our mentors, in different aspects of our lives; as well as having also met people who have disappointed us because of their incongruity and at the moment of truth, have revealed themselves as nothing but smoke sellers.

Unfortunately there are many "coaches" today who give you the keys to success, but when you look at their lives, you would like to recommend that they apply those same keys to themselves. I once heard the great Tony Robbins say: "don't watch the lips move, watch the feet move and the path traveled." The first recommendation that I will make is that you don't follow the advice of someone who doesn't have the results you are looking for in their own life. That being the case, when someone recommends an investment, ask him or her if he or she invests in that product they are recommending and ask them to show you the results they have obtained. In the same way, if they recommend a financial plan or keys to success, ask them what results they have, after having applied that plan and those keys.

Take this book as a practical guide. There will be tips that you can apply immediately and others that you will dismiss outright. You'll leave some others for later and in a second reading, perhaps in a few months or years, you will rediscover them, realizing that now is your time.

Our wish is that this helps you achieve a prosperous and limitless life on your own terms.

PART ONE

A NEW FINANCIAL CONSCIOUSNESS

CASHFLOW, CASHFLOW, CASHFLOW.

$

Will I be rich or poor? What does the future hold for me? Will I be successful? Oh, crystal ball... tell me, what will become of me?... I will try to throw this wad of paper into the trash can... if I make it, I'll be rich, if I miss, I'll be poor... mhmm... I missed... fine... 2 out of 3 tries... or ¿3 out of 5??? Come on... admit it!... We've all done it!

Many people believe that they're adrift and have no control over their lives or futures. As we've talked about it, they are like Forrest Gump's feather in the movie just waiting to see where the wind blows. Since they have no idea how the laws of money work and have no plan to prosper, in their mind they don't understand how they'll become rich, so they delegate the possibility of being rich to luck.

I want to tell you that we can predict our economic future. It doesn't depend on a crystal ball or you throwing another piece of paper into the trash can. It depends on two things; the first is your monthly cashflow, meaning, how much you have left at the end of the month after earning and spending. The second depends on your ability to invest that money wisely, finding good rates of return with low or moderate risk. We'll talk about that second skill later because it becomes relevant only when you have done a good job of generating monthly cashflow.

When we read books on financial intelligence, Americans, experts in making money, repeat over and over again: cashflow, cashflow, cashflow ... cashflow, that stream of cash that you have every month, free to save and invest. The seed of money is money. If you don't have seeds to plant, you can't harvest. If at the end of the month you have nothing left or worse, you spend more than what you earn and you get into debt, you won't be able to save in order to invest.

Let me make this very clear for you:

NO CASHFLOW = NO POSSIBILITY OF FINANCIAL FREEDOM

This is where one of the most important principles of financial intelligence comes from, *It doesn't matter how much you make, what matters is how much you have left at the end of the month;* as we will see in depth in the chapter "It's time to... Increase your income!" There is a general idea in the collective unconsciousness and it is a terrible lie; this idea is to believe that if you make more money, you will solve your financial problems. Whoever makes 1000, believes that if they could only win 1500 or 2000, than everything would be solved. Whoever wins 2000 believes that the solution is 3000, whoever wins 5000 wants 7000 and we can continue giving examples up to any figure.

It has been proven that when a person increases their income, in the next 60-90 days their expenses increase in the same proportion or more. There is even a law that talks about this, which is called Parkinson's Second Law:

> *"Expenditures or "money paid" out rises to meet income."- Cyril Northcote Parkinson (Historian, University Professor and Writer of more than 60 books)*

Check it out and you will see; it's pure statistics. How is that possible? First, the obvious: by increasing your income, the cost you pay for social security and taxes also increases. On the other hand, your mind adjusts to the new figure and since we don't have a mentality of prosperity, we find how to make use of that excess in the fastest and almost always inefficient way. Your ego increases with your income, making you feel worthy of more luxurious and expensive things.

You will see proportionally lower prices compared to what you earn and that will drive you to spend more. To your mind, It is not the same when a watch costs $1500 dollars and your income is $2.000 that when your income is $5.000. I remember one time we traveled with my wife Cata, many years ago, to the Dominican Republic. We were going to give a series of paid lectures on entrepreneurship, all expenses paid. It was one of our first experiences as international speakers. The flight we were on was stopping in Panama for a couple of hours and we wanted to buy a new television, knowing that this country is known for its good tax-free prices. On the outbound flight, we checked the televisions at the airport stores and I remember that they seemed very expensive. So much so, that we said it was silly to shop there and were disappointed with our expectations of finding a good bargain. After the successful tour, we returned with a stop-off at the same airport in Panama, just a few days later. On the way to our gate we passed the same stores and saw the same televisions at the same prices. However, something had changed: we had in our pockets the money from the fees that we had been paid for the conference. We lived an incredible phenomenon. Now the televisions seemed cheaper to me than before, when they seemed expensive. Did the store prices change? No. What changed was the ratio of what the television cost vs. what we had in our pockets. On the way out, I only had a few dollars for emergencies and the television could be 4 times what I had in my pockets. On the way back, we had 5 times the cost of the television in our pockets. I remember feeling an irresistible urge to buy it and telling my wife Cata that it was at a very good price. I tried to justify the purchase by referring to things like the features it had, the quality of the image and anything else I could think of. Fortunately, Cata is more financially savvy than I am in that sort of thing and she avoided the purchase, insisting that nothing had changed. The experiment, however, was very interesting, because we could see in a very short time how the perception of the value of things had changed. This is what happens when you earn more, and that's why it's inevitable: you tend to spend more, whether it makes sense or not.

This phenomenon usually affects changes in the place where you live, the car you drive, the size of your TV, the distance and category of vacations you take and the amount of things your family does and buys. Is there a problem with us giving ourselves and our family the best things? Of course not. The problem is if you do it ahead of time and especially if you still don't have a positive cashflow. We are excited to help you discover the power of compound interest and the enormous wealth that cashflow will bring into your life. We'll reveal it to you soon and everything we've said so far will make sense. For now, understand that the priority is to generate free cashflow in order to save for investments and begin to build your personal freedom (and that of your family).

It is important to establish a financial action plan, with your partner and children, if you have them, so that they understand what you're doing and why you shouldn't increase your expenses in line with your income. Don't you want them to understand and support you, everyone trying hard as a family in the present, so that you can have an unlimited future and above all a future of freedom? Think that those seeds that you sow in your present with your cashflow, will be what in the future you will reap as assets (businesses, properties, intellectual property), which will produce money and thus, the safety of your family will not depend on whether you work or not. That money from assets will make it easier to spend more time in enjoying with your family, which is much more important and significant than a short-term pleasure or even the purchase of an object that will soon lose its value.

- **"We will do this in order to be secure and calm in the future."**

- **"I want your support in this financial plan so that we can spend more time together and give our family the best."**

- **"By following this plan as a family, we will avoid having to worry about chasing after money for the rest of our lives."**

- **"I want to spend more time with you."**

- **"I want us to work, being focused on achieving what we want, and to avoid what happens to most people who work for their entire lives and end up with nothing."**

- "I have a plan that gives us the security we want in the future, to avoid being dependent on a pension or state security. This plan requires effort in the present but guarantees us peace of mind."

The above are phrases that will help you start these conversations with your family. Note that we never mention the word "sacrifices." We speak of "efforts." A sacrifice involves giving something in exchange for nothing. An effort encourages you to give something in exchange for something greater. Nothing we propose has to do with sacrifice. It has to do with effort and it's important that you and your family understand it.

What if they still don't understand it? Then you will have to be firm and make decisions, since it is evident that they still don't understand what is clear to you: Your future and that of your family is in your hands and how you handle your present time.

Talking frankly and openly about money is important. Removing the social taboo that it entails, is vital in order to face and become better on money issues. It's logical right? If you can't even talk about it, then how would you even improve it? Many people have limiting beliefs when it comes to expressing their feelings about money. Money is neither good nor bad. Money is energy. Money is a magnifying glass that shows what is inside you. Imagine a person who has addictions such as alcohol and gambling. Will having more money make their life better? Of course not, it will get them into more trouble. For sure, they'll end up worse, gambling and generating larger debts than they previously had. If a kind and caring person has a lot of money, then they can help many people. If an evil person, for example a terrorist, has a lot of money, they'll only cause lots of deaths and a lot of pain. It's not the money, but the hand that uses it. It is the mind that moves that hand. It's what's in the heart. That is why we recommend that all our students work on themselves, that they grow as human beings, and that they develop empathy and love for others. We want you to have all the money in the world and we also want you to be the best person you can be. If we are many with good intentions and with a lot of money, we can do a lot for this planet and for others.

I'm excited to see how several billionaires are coming together to solve humanity's greatest problems. One example is the Bill & Melinda Gates foundation, supported by magnate Warren Buffet. They have allocated huge funds to attack the roots of problems such as health in Africa, clean water, the fight against AIDS and other diseases or the generation of clean and renewable energy. Also in the COVID19 pandemic they have donated sums of hundreds of millions of dollars for the development of vaccines and treatments.

We are going to share with you what we have done in our own lives to improve that monthly cashflow and this way dispose of seeds of prosperity that over time have germinated and today have given us a life without limits. In the next chapters, we will show the power that this positive cashflow has in the design of your future. You will see how it doesn't have to be huge. With a little bit each month, you can create wealth. Of course, as you prosper, you can increase the cashflow with an increasingly larger cashflow each time and this will speed up your pace and shorten the times.

For now, let's dive into the controversial topic of saving and let's answer the important question that the next chapter is entitled with.

IS IT WORTH SAVING TODAY?

My grandmother gave me my first piggy bank. It was made out of red plastic in the shape of a little house; they would give it away for free at a well-known and popular bank in order for the children to learn how to save. With it, came advice from the elders about how I could buy whatever I wanted, if I saved. They also explained to us how if we left the money in the bank they would give us interest that would increase the amount of money we had.

The concept was that you lent your money to the bank and the bank worked with your money, that is, it lent it to others and charged them more than they paid you. The fact that they paid you something made it interesting to save, and with time and with the payment of interest on interest, which is called compound interest (we will talk about in the next chapter) you could get a significant capital.

With the passing of time, the banks influences governments to have carte blanche and print money, without being required to support new loans with real assets. At the beginning, by law, the bank could only lend 10 times what it had in people's savings. Today it is practically infinite. For this reason, they no longer need your savings and have substituted interest for administrative fees and charges for transfers, withdrawals or similar things. In short, they have discouraged saving and most people today don't see any sense in doing it, since they perceive that there is no reward for the effort to limit their expenses. I remember the Economics class in which the professor told us: higher interests equals greater savings, lower interests brings more spending.

Well, the teacher was right. Savings levels are today the lowest in history and the new generations have the shocking figure of zero savings. Today, most young people are not saving. Studies also show that the few who save don't do so with the goal of investing those savings or creating security, but do it to pay off debts and go on vacation. It is unfortunate. In Europe, older generations were used to living on a percentage of what they earned, many with half of it. With the very long winters, plagues, world wars and catastrophes, wisdom relied in saving for the months of need and retirement. This makes a lot of sense now in the face of the situation generated by the pandemic, right? History tends to repeat itself and surely this global situation will create a consciousness that will rescue those grandparents wisdom.

Today, governments with their pension and social security plans, especially in the "welfare states", convinced the majority that it's not necessary to save since "the state will take care of you, even when you lose your job" ... Big mistake!, because that system has collapsed and our planet is overpopulated. There isn't enough for everyone, so the states go into debt non-stop, and each time more and more people are in crisis, without stable work and without an adequate pension for their elder population. In top of that, longevity is higher than ever, therefore it is easy to understand why there are more and more pension reforms, that just want you to work longer for less money.

Faced with a crisis as big as that of the new coronavirus, all of this got much worse. Governments issued lots of decrees with figures of billions for financial bailouts and to help those in need. They do this with money they don't have, meaning, they generate more debt that in turn causes new taxes and more inflation, and ends up being paid by the citizens of the countries, which are becoming poorer, while their money is worth less every year.

Betting on traditional systems or States and not taking responsibility for ensuring your future is a serious mistake. The global situation in this moment is easier to understand than we think: the systems with which governments operate are obsolete and weren't created for today's population or for current conditions.

I'll make it easy for you to understand, by the year 1800 we were a billion people on the planet. It took humanity hundreds of thousands of years to reach that population. By 1927 we were two billion, twice as large. The projection for 2023 is 8 Billion and for 2030 its 8.5, that is, we will experience a growth of a Billion people in 10 years, the same amount that we reached in almost the entire history of humanity. Most governments apply systems created and designed for when we were only a billion people on the planet and also lived half the years we live today, on average. Do a simple exercise, multiply by 8 the number of people who live in your house. If you are alone, imagine that there were 8 in the same space. If there are 4, imagine it would be 32. Take a minute or two to think about what the living conditions would be like? Would there be a crisis? What kind? Financial? Environmental? Waste generation? Everything would collapse, wouldn't it? Well, that is precisely what happens on our planet and in the systems, do you see it now? The health, retirement, education, employment, judicial, and transportation systems are outdated and the changes that are being made aren't going at the rate in which the world is changing. The only solution to keep these obsolete systems is to increase the debt levels that are already at historical levels. There is no political party, world leader or economic system that can reverse it, it is up to each and every one of us to become responsible and take charge of ourselves and of our own; expecting otherwise is insane.

The 2020 pandemic came to show us how fragile we are and how weak the government structures are in all countries. The repercussions of this will be immense and will take many years to dissolve. Time that won't be enough before the next great global situation arrives affecting the planet either environmentally, socially, economically or health wise, with the appearance of another virus.

What do you think? It's a dark panorama for the traditional right? And we haven't even talked about what's coming! I recommend that you read "The robots are coming", by the journalist Andrés Oppenheimer, who tells us how with the massive entry of artificial intelligence and robots, the world bank is expecting that in the short term around 47% of existing jobs in the United States and 57% in Europe will disappear. The figure for Latin America is even more alarming at 67%. These jobs will be done by machines in a much more efficient and cheaper way. We're not talking only about automatic jobs, but about professions with the highest degrees of sophistication, such as strategic planning, psychology, law and surgical medicine.

The most complicated thing is that we're not prepared as a species to face the changes that are coming and the speed with which they will occur. Most people are sitting comfortably on the couch watching TV or behind a computer screen, complaining to others that everything is getting worse and doing nothing to change their situation. With modern life, food preservation and the perception that nothing can go wrong because I have public services, Wi-Fi and a supermarket on the corner, a microwave mentality has set in that we want everything immediately and effortlessly.

We hope that the current crisis situation generated by the Coronavirus pandemic and the innumerable discomforts and restrictions to which we have been subjected to, will help us to change our mentality and wake us up, understanding that we must adapt to changes, otherwise as Darwin said, we will not survive. For many years we have seen humanity sleepy and well-off, mired in a collective hypnosis very similar to that of the movie Matrix, where computers had human beings connected to machines and people spent their lives experiencing a false reality. We think that something as shocking as what we've experienced with the pandemic will help many people wake up, live their lives with intensity and take responsibility for their finances and their future. Unfortunately, we know that statistically, within time many will forget it and once again go back into zombie mode, only poorer than they were before the pandemic.

There is a sad popular saying and it is that "human beings get used to everything" and as the great Tony Robbins says, in life we don't get what we dream of or what we want, but instead what we are willing to tolerate. Most get used to very low standards of living and are willing to tolerate mediocrity. In fact, it has been proven that, in most cases, no matter what situation occurs, no matter how painful or traumatic it is, no matter the ecstasy and happiness that a certain event produces, in a matter of 90 days you will have gotten used to this new situation and it will seem normal to you. From an extreme situation like the sudden loss of all your capital to another like winning the lottery; in 3 months, you will have gotten used to that new reality.

In our conferences and whenever we share with groups, we have assumed the task of sharing this global economic reality with them and asking them to open their eyes and understand today's world. We tell them to stop expecting the impossible: for someone else to take care of them. We encourage them to take up something new and take charge of their financial future without wasting any more time; because the sooner they start, the faster they will prosper and will stop being part of the vulnerable population, which is increasing.

So let's get to work ... let's answer the question:

Is It Worth Saving?

Given the situation unleashed in 2020, we are sure that for you it's already obvious that we have to prepare our finances for extreme situations. However, even under normal conditions, our answer is yes, as long as you do so backed by a financial plan. That financial plan should have several stages, starting with security and progressing to wealth. The first thing we teach in the workshops is to build a financial cushion, based on savings, to protect you in times of need. That mattress, or as some call it, "airbag" or financial lifejacket, will be your backup fund to cover at least six months to a year of your expenses. The bigger the fund, the better; if job stability is low and there are less job offers in your sector, the more months of provisions there should be. The longer it takes to get back to work after leaving a job, the more months covered by the fund. This savings aren't to become rich, but to sleep peacefully at night. It's so that you have something to hold on to and your family is secure, for at least 6 months to 1 year of covered expenses, while you solve the problem. This fund is also the one that will cover you in the moments when you cannot work and have no income for whatever reason, such as illness, confinement due to pollution, pandemic, closure of the company you worked for or end of the industry in which you were developing. Find it dramatic? It no longer seems dramatic to us after what we've experienced in 2020, isn't that true?

After the events experienced in recent times, many people now understand how important it is to have this emergency fund. Unfortunately, it is already too late for many of them, at least to face the crisis they are going through. The news shows that most freelancers are just a month away from ruin. Perhaps they'll learn their lesson and better prepare for the next one, you can always start over. With thousands of lost jobs and many independent workers unable to leave their homes due to the pandemic, many wish they had anticipated and built up their financial cushion that would have given them and their family's financial peace of mind at this time. The pandemic prompted many to reassess their priorities. It's important to understand that an emergency fund has more value than a luxury car paid in installments. True financial security is more important than social status and "what neighbors think."

Once you have your complete financial lifejacket, you can start to allocate your savings to more interesting things, such as an ETF fund (exchange-traded fund, a hybrid between an investment fund and a stock fund), not actively managed. Without high transactions fees and commissions, every month you contribute a fixed sum and even in the face of the ups and downs of the stock market, over time it will grow, since you are betting on the largest companies of the strongest economies; An example is the S&P500 (Standard and Poor´s) index fund, which is equivalent to buying a piece of the 500 largest companies in the United States. Also, if one of these companies in which you invested that small chunk is no longer among the 500 largest, it is immediately replaced. You can also start creating a real estate investment fund, our favorite investment product and what we've learned to do in a professional way. Furthermore, as you increase your financial intelligence, you will see how each month more money will be left, allowing you to invest in different assets types; some will work and some won't, but the ones that work can generate huge returns on your investment. However, we are getting ahead of ourselves and this isn't a book on investment advice, although we will share a few. Take the above as an example that saving is worth it when you do it with a purpose. That purpose, also, is not to pay off debts or go on vacation, or buy a new car. Purpose has to do with first creating stability and security in your life, then investing and building wealth at rapid speed. We're not talking about savings to leave in the bank or to have there for a lifetime. We are talking about savings that will become seeds that you will plant in an increasingly fertile ground.

The best financial mentors like Kiyosaki himself say that "Saving is for losers", that it's not worth it, which can be misinterpreted. What this phrase really means, and with which we agree, is that it's not worth saving if you're not going to do something with that money. It's worth saving if you're going to invest.

The tips shared in this book will allow you to generate cashflow that will become the water that irrigates your investment plants. Think of it like this... imagine you have a beautiful garden with different types of plants and flowers, and you have a hose to spray the plants with. If it's disconnected from the water source, there isn't much you can do to make your plants grow and be healthy. That is the equivalent of not saving and not having cashflow, the hose has no purpose. Now imagine that you connect the hose but instead of directing the water at the plants you direct it to the drainage system. Well that is the equivalent of saving without a financial plan. Lastly, imagine the connected hose and a good cashflow of water spraying your plants. They'll grow big and strong, and since you have a vast variety, it'll be a beautiful garden. That is what we're prompting, that you save (connect the hose), and direct your cashflow to various types of investments (spraying different plants), some will give you security, others will generate freedom because they'll make money monthly so that you can live without working; others will just make you rich.

COMPOUND INTEREST AND WHY YOU CAN DREAM BIG

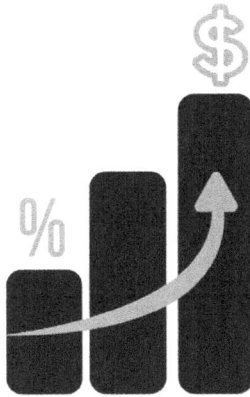

N ow that we have answered the question of whether saving is worth it, let's get into the most exciting part, and that is how with just a few dollars saved up each month you can turn it into a fortune by increasing your financial intelligence. Brace yourself and fasten your seatbelt, as the information in this chapter may be the most revealing and exciting thing you have ever come across in financial terms. At least that's how it was for us.

Many authors who write about money refer to Compound Interest as millionaires' best-kept secret. It's an exciting topic; it's like turning your money into a slave who goes out energized, to get you more money. In this chapter we'll make sure you understand it, value it, and become a compound interest hunter for life. Many years ago we discovered, how by saving a dollar a day at a good interest rate for 65 years, you could produce a capital of more than a billion dollars. This discovery has had a huge impact on our lives.

Interest refers to the cost of money. It is how much it costs you to borrow a sum of money. For example, an interest of 5% per year means that for every 100 dollars that you borrow, you assume a cost of 5 dollars per year. It is a cost that the debtor bears with the lender. The key is to be the lender and not the debtor. When you are the lender, it doesn't cost you $5 instead you earn $5 a year.

What is compound interest? It is charging interest on interest. There is one that makes you poor which we will call "toxic compound interest", and there is also one that makes you immensely wealthy, we'll call it the "magical compound interest."

A practical example: You have $1,000 and you put it in an investment that pays you a fixed interest of 10%. In a year you will have 1100 dollars with a profit of an additional 100 to your initial capital of 1000. If you leave it there and the second year you earn the same interest, now they'll pay you over the 1100 and you will earn 110. For the second year, you'll have 1210 dollars in capital and your profit will be $121 in the third year. In 7 years you will have doubled your money, in 20 you will have multiplied it by 7, in 31 years by 20 and in 40 years you will have 53 times your initial capital, even if you never make a contribution again. Now, if instead of 10% you get 20%, you will have almost 400,000 in 30 years and a little less than 3 million dollars in 40 years. You will accumulate all this money by allocating just $1,000 only once in your life. Imagine that at 25 years of age, you choose to insure your old age and allocate 1,000 dollars for it. What will happen, is that at the age of your retirement you will have a fortune thanks to that return. There are several variables that affect how rich you will be: 1)

The amount you contribute, 2) how often you do it, 3) how long your investment lasts, and 4) the interest you earn. We will talk more about this later.

Toxic Compound Interest is generated when you are the debtor; for example, it's the interest they charge you for purchases made with credit cards. A common mistake is making installment payments with your credit card. If you buy some $360 shoes and put it on 36 months, you think you will only pay $10 a month and that's it, easy! You won't even notice and you'll have your shoes. The problem is that the bank charges you interest and those on credit cards are usually the highest in the market. Of course, the amount you will pay for your shoes will be higher; you will pay interest on interest, that is, the costs of credit will generate more costs. That's why if you are a frequent user of credit cards, you may feel like you pay and pay and the debt never goes down. If we add the handling fee, the management fees associated with the cards, the insurance they often include and the hidden costs, you can end up paying $800 for a $200 credit card payment! Toxic without a doubt; it impoverishes you and turns you into a modern slave of banks.

Not only will magical compound interest give you security and prosperity, it also has the potential of making you rich, or better yet ... MEGA RICH. It's about starting to send your money to bring in more money. Some attendees of our talks or readers of our posts on compound interest get confused and think they should go to their bank and ask for financial products of compound interest. Bank employees who don't understand anything about investment get confused, because they don't know what you're are talking about.

And how do I invest with compound interest?

We know that this is a topic that causes a lot of interest, but also a lot of confusion. Also, we have seen that some take advantage of the term "compound interest", selling financial products as if they were exclusive to generate it, when the reality is that any investment can generate compound interest, so if you follow this QR code, you will find a video that explains it in detail.

Repetition is the mother of all skills, as I will repeat to you several times in the book. I'll tell you again: any investment, be it real estate, financial papers, stocks or simple loans, can generate earnings because of compound interests. Any investment has compound interest if you are patient. It works when you have a profit on an investment, your capital increases and you don't use that investment nor that profit, instead you leave it there so that now you continue to earn not only on your investment, but also on the profits that it had already produced; as we saw in the practical example a couple of paragraphs above. We are going to do some examples to make this clearer, because the best way to see the potential is to see the numbers.

	INTEREST RATE			
$ 100	5%	8%	12%	18%
5	$ 6.829	$ 7.397	$ 8.249	$ 9.766
10	$ 15.593	$ 18.417	$ 23.234	$ 33.626
20	$ 41.275	$ 59.295	$ 99.915	$ 234.349
30	$ 83.573	$ 150.030	$ 352.991	$ 1.432.529

Here we show an example of a saving of 100 dollars per month, it's the same. If you convert it to a daily value, we are talking about 3 dollars a day. Today there are very elegant coffee shops, where you can order something like "a special double latte macchiato espresso". That many words used to define the fancy coffee you want, are accompanied by overcharges to the price, and it's normal for people to pay more than 3 dollars for their coffee. If you're going to have coffee as a couple, it is already 6 or more dollars. Maybe $3 doesn't sound like much to you, but that daily coffee has something associated with it called "opportunity cost." Opportunity cost, we were taught in economics, is what you stop earning for making a choice. For example, let's say you have to choose one of two possible investments, one is real estate and the other is a mutual fund. In the first, you get an income of 6% per year, plus a property valuation and tax benefits. In the second you get a fixed 8%. It may be that at first glance it is better to go for 8% of the mutual fund, but by making that choice you are missing the opportunity to earn the additional benefits of investing in real estate and that comes at a cost. You will find that under normal conditions, due to the valuation of the properties, it is better to invest in real estate at 6% than in financial papers at 8%. To put it in simple words that connect with us, the "opportunity cost" is equivalent to the "if I had".

A mentor once told us that, hell was reaching the end of your days and meeting the person you could have been. That certainly changed our life. Why? Because the opportunity cost of not making decisions or the action necessary to change our lives was very high. It meant missing out on that improved version of ourselves. Most people don't understand that not making a decision is also making a decision, because when you don't choose, you are choosing to miss out on everything that your life had in store for you (opportunity cost).

Whether or not you drink coffee, may seem like an insignificant decision, but if you look at this table you can understand the opportunity cost associated with that decision. You will see how after 5, 10, 20 or 30 years, depending on the interest you have obtained, you'll get figures that are increasing. For example, if you are 25 years old, and you use that daily coffee expense instead for your financial future and your freedom fund, with an annual interest of 18%, after 30 years, at 55, you will have accumulated a capital of almost a million and a half dollars. Believe me that the vast majority of people in your country and on the planet, at the age of 55 years or older, don't have a figure of that value in their assets and never will; All with the money it costs for a coffee a day, a few cigarettes, a sugary drink or a beer. Don't you dare call it a sacrifice... it's an effort and the prize you get is a million and a half bigger! It´s a 1 million dollar coffee!

All of us who live in normal conditions can save. Some may save more than others, and the starting point may be different. The problem isn't in the ability to save but in the motivation and values that move a person to do so. Many see the act of depriving themselves of some foolish and fleeting pleasure as a restriction and loss of freedom in their life. They aren't looking at this table and they aren't having perspective or understanding what precisely needs to be done in order to achieve true freedom. Do it because that fortune, the fruit of that minimum daily effort, will allow you to be free! Imagine a life without time or money limitations ... working or not, at your choice, spending time doing what you love and being with the people with whom you want to share your life with, supporting the causes that move your heart and, in general, living your life with passion and energy.

Now, let's go a little further. Let's say that you choose to make a plan based on what you will learn in this book and that you can, starting this month, save not 100 but 200 dollars per month. Even with the simplest interest you could buy one or more properties with that capital (depending on where you live) and put them up for rent. Not to mention the results you will get if you become a professional investor and learn to achieve high rates of return on your investments. In this case, 18% would produce you a delicious almost 3 million dollars!

	$ 200	INTEREST RATE			
		5%	8%	12%	18%
YEARS	5	$ 13.658	$ 14.793	$ 16.497	$ 19.532
	10	$ 31.186	$ 36.833	$ 46.468	$ 67.252
	20	$ 82.549	$ 118.589	$ 199.830	$ 468.697
	30	$ 167.145	$ 300.059	$ 705.983	$ 2.865.058

What'll happen if you continue applying the tips that you will learn in this book? Well, it will increase your cashflow. Now you begin to understand why we said cashflow, cashflow, cashflow! Because the more cashflow, the faster you'll become rich and in greater quantity. See in our following table how everything changes with a 500 dollars of monthly savings, destined for investment. And how can you get that? Well, by applying the keys that you'll see in the next chapters and applying yourself as a good student of financial intelligence.

A simple venture can be the source of money that allows you to start saving this figure per month, generating a small extra cashflow of income, without affecting your current finances. I want you to look at those figures in the table and see them as if they were already yours! What would you do with 750,000 dollars? What would you do with 7 million dollars? What would your life be like? Do you know that, in addition, since you'll be an investment master, it's possible that you'll be able to make a tremendous profit from that money, leaving you about 60 thousand dollars a month in income? Go figure! Most people would achieve the life of their dreams with a quarter of that. So why limit yourself if compound interest lets you dream big?

		INTEREST RATE			
	$ 500	5%	8%	12%	18%
YEARS	5	$ 34.145	$ 36.983	$ 41.243	$ 48.829
	10	$ 77.965	$ 92.083	$ 116.170	$ 168.129
	20	$ 206.373	$ 296.474	$ 499.574	$ 1.171.744
	30	$ 417.863	$ 750.148	$ 1.764.957	$ 7.162.645

Now let's go to a more interesting figure: 1000 dollars per month savings for investment. What I want you to understand is that this figure is within your reach with the series of tips that you will receive to increase your cashflow. They will require a mixture of actions that will include reducing your unnecessary expenses, but above all increasing your income with entrepreneurships. The point is to create a money-making machine that will eventually allow you to not only stop working if you wish to and cover all your expenses, but also produce an extra amount that you can take advantage of to generate a powerful and accelerated compound interest.

Look at how in the following table, times are shortened and the figures are increased with 1000 dollars per month. It is our last table, because now you'll be able to make your own, and if you go follow the QR code at the end of this chapter and click on the compound interest calculator, you'll be able to project with the figures you want, at the timeframe you choose and with the interest you decide. Hey ... It's worth dreaming! Put high numbers and project what could happen when you have a big cashflow. Dreaming is good, do it big! I'll anticipate something ... if you project the table with figures of 5000 or 10,000, you could reach more than 150 million in capital! There's no limit to what you can achieve in time if you become a professional investor and a cashflow generator!

		INTEREST RATE			
	$ 1.000	5%	8%	12%	18%
YEARS	5	$ 68.289	$ 73.967	$ 82.486	$ 97.658
	10	$ 155.929	$ 184.166	$ 232.339	$ 336.258
	20	$ 412.746	$ 592.947	$ 999.148	$ 2.343.487
	30	$ 835.726	$ 1.500.295	$ 3.529.914	$ 14.325.289

Years ago, once we understood the value of this information, we began to greatly value the money that we managed to keep at the end of the month. At first we did it with little, but as our income increased, we chose to keep our expenses stable in that proportion. We also raised our quality of life to a certain extent, but above all we increased our investment cashflow. With discipline, patience, and confidence in the process, the numbers in those tables have become reality for us. It hasn't been overnight, I repeat: with patience and strategy. Getting rich is a matter of strategy. It's not a stroke of luck, it's a plan. Do you find it boring? Do you want something more dizzying? Well then, maybe wealth isn't for you; maybe it's better that you dedicate yourself to buying the lottery or looking for gold and diamonds in the rivers of Africa, because the rich, in the vast majority of cases, build their wealth this way.

Every prize in life has a price to pay. The relationship between these two words is impressive, not only because of the change from the "z" in priZe to the "c" in priCe. The price of real and lasting wealth is paid with consistency and discipline. Soap operas and the disastrous series of drug traffickers have made most people think that wealth is achieved quickly, with a successful shipment. This mentality is one of the most atrocious consequences that the scourge of drug trafficking has produced, as it has made people think that what they have to do is look for "shortcuts" and get-rich-quick schemes. Unfortunately, we have seen that those who take these "shortcuts" end up paying a much higher price, many times ending with their lives, in jail or with the total destruction of their families. It's not worth it, because in any case, even if you manage to escape from all that, you'll end up living with yourself, and I don't think you're good company if that's the way you make your money.

Do you want to make your own calculations?

We imagine that you are excited about the potential of compound interest; In the following QR code you will be able to do your own simulations, based on the figures that you can save today and those that you'll be able to earn in the future, after doing the tasks that this book presents.

IS SAVING POSSIBLE?
HACK YOUR BIOLOGY

A fter verifying that it's worth saving if it's done for the purpose of investing and understanding that from this the seed of wealth is born, we have a second question to answer regarding whether it's possible to do so.

In our workshops and conferences, we see people all the time who have every intention of starting to save. As it happens with everything in real life, the intention isn't enough. Same thing happens if someone, with the intention of learning a language, enrolls in the course and then doesn't go to the classes.

These people intended on saving after having finished the course, leave the first month, only with their intention, they earn, spend and then want to save. They realize that something happened and they were left with no money at the end of the month, so they promise themselves that next month they will. With a little more awareness, again they go with their intention, they earn, they spend (a little less because of their intention to save), but then something unexpected happens, like the washer machine getting damaged, the car having to go to the shop or any of these that should be budgeted in any case, as they are maintenance and expenses that may occur; but by living their financial lives as a series of unplanned events, they run out of money and finally, again, they don't save. The third month, same thing happens and then they label themselves and say to themselves "I can't save", throwing all their savings and freedom plans out the window. When you believe that phrase and identify yourself as someone who "cannot", you are condemning yourself, and the consequences are dire. This is the consequence of not knowing the keys behind a good saver.

In this chapter we will address two of the most important concepts that we have learned over the years and that have allowed us to save in order to invest thousands and tens and hundreds of thousands of dollars over the years. Mastering these two concepts has been essential. They are the most basic of all the basic steps. You'll find them in every respectable book on money management and financial intelligence. Now we will tell you about our interpretation and application of these principles and how you can start doing it this month. We will also add to the equation something that we consider to be vital and that is our own biology.

Principle No. 1: Hack Your Brain. Put Your Future First And Pay Yourself First.

This principle is very easy to explain, but applying it requires vision and discipline. What it involves is simply changing the order of things and unlike the commutative law learned in school, here the order of factors does alter the product. What we'll do is replace:

Earn > Spend > Save

for

Earn > Save > Spend

It's impressive the impact that applying this simple formula can have on your financial life. You'll no longer have the problem that after spending you're left without money left and you can't save. Now you will save as soon as you receive your income and thus ensuring that you'll meet your goal; sending that percentage that you've allocated to savings into a low liquidity trust account, giving it to someone you trust with whom you've made a pact with that they'll keep it for you or having a Automatic investment plan that debits you once your income is deposited each month.

Experts agree in recommending a minimum saving of 10% of your income. This percentage can vary according to your age and your financial goals. However, don't get overwhelmed with that just yet, the important thing is to start. Let's put it in numbers with an example in which you earn 2,000 dollars per month and you have the goal of saving that 10%.

Profit = 2,000
Savings (10%) = -200
Expense = 1800

I can hear your reptilian mind (the one in charge of fear and survival) jumping up and saying I can't do that! I need those $200, what if $1800 is not enough? Well, if what you want is freedom and financial intelligence, here is a secret: it is better that you make your subconscious mind uncomfortable and not let it reach you. Our brain is divided into three; it's almost like having three brains in one. The first is the reptilian brain, which is the most primitive and we have so much to thank it for, since it has kept us as a species to this day. If it weren't for this brain, we wouldn't have survived the ice age nor the saber tooth tigers, as well as many other predators that would have wiped us out. This brain is the one that causes us stress and fear every time it feels threatened. It is very sensitive to money issues, as it considers it to be vital for us to survive. This brain is surrounded by the mammalian or emotional brain which is the second brain, and finally we have the cortex or human brain, the logical part of our brain, our third brain. When the reptilian brain feels threatened, it has the ability to hack the other 2 and seeks to take control. This brain doesn't care about things like love, happiness, personal growth, quality of life, and financial freedom. Its task is to have you alive to see tomorrow, just as it did hundreds of thousands of years ago.

When we make the brain uncomfortable, it dedicates itself to looking for what we need: solutions. If, for example, before applying the principle No. 1 of saving before spending, you spent 2,000 a month, now you will have a shortage of those 200 that you are now saving and your brain will have a good problem to solve. I say "good", because the reason you are doing all of this is to be free and prosperous, don't forget! Remember, it is effort and not sacrifice. Just as there are bad debts and good debts, which we will talk about in the debt chapter, there are bad problems and good problems. Bad problems are those that attend to the urgent and good problems aim to achieve something important. Spending all day thinking about how to pay rent and bills is a bad problem, because ultimately, when you solve it, you're not building anything for yourself and you're using all your energy and time, which are valuable resources. The solutions to bad problems are usually poor, like borrowing from someone or earning some money from an activity where you don't build any assets. That doesn't mean that you don't have to attend to it, of course you do, but if you stay there you'll only have those problems your whole life and you'll live in a repetitive cycle, every month looking for solutions. On the contrary, when you solve good problems, they'll solve the bad ones for life. If you solve the problem of generating those extra 200 that you lack, with an asset (business or investment), you will never worry about them again.

The reason you can't save using the Earn>Expenses>Savings formula is because your brain is comfortable. Your reptilian brain doesn't see the need to save because you've got today covered. I imagine you watching TV calmly and with your brain anesthetized, without looking for any solution to the fact that you won't be able to save this month. In the third month, you throw in the towel because for your brain you never had the real need to do it and that's why you never found the energy to do so.

When you make your brain uncomfortable, by having an unshakable goal of saving, you hack it so that now you'll have the ideas and the energy to solve it. For example, you'll start up something new, put more energy towards your current venture, learn more about an investment, and expand your knowledge and your financial intelligence. Why? Because now it's a necessity. Here is something that, perhaps, will sound strange to you: Don't be afraid to be afraid. It's just what you need to get into action.

If you're still thinking that you can't do it, ask yourself this simple question. What would happen if the government of your country created a new tax or law, from which they would withhold an additional 10% of your income because there is a deficit to cover? That is, if before receiving your salary, companies were required to retain an additional 10% and you received less in your monthly or biweekly payment. What would you do? You would have to adjust, right? And why would you do it for your government, who knows what these funds will be used for and that, ultimately, it is very likely that your life won't change at all, and not do it for yourself, for your future and that of your family? You are the president of your life, the king of your experience on this earth. Create a mental decree, a new law in your life in which every month there is a retention with a wonderful destiny: your freedom and that of your family. But ... do it with good energy. You shouldn't do it as if it were a burden; it has to be something positive and emotionally significant. Think that you are doing all this to have a spectacular quality of life. Imagine already being in that desired future. Visualize yourself and your family living that incredible life that is awaiting you. This little financial reengineering that you are doing cannot be compared to the prize that you're going to receive, the satisfaction you will have and how proud you will be of yourself. Also, after reading the chapter on compound interest, you already know that that's how it'll be. So, get excited and be passionate about your action plan and your future.

Principle No. 2: Delayed gratification and our hormones.

"The wealthy buy luxuries last, while the poor and middle-class tend to buy luxuries first."- R. Kiyosaki

This principle was one of the most important we learned on our journey in building wealth. It means that the prize is given to you when you win it, when you meet the goal, not when you're tired or frustrated and need to give yourself a little contentment to fill a void.

Marketing takes advantage of our frustrations and convinces us that we can fill our internal voids with external things. If you bought a certain watch, you would feel elegant; if you had a certain car, you would be free; if you go on vacation to a certain place, you will be happy; with a certain brand of clothing, you would be powerful and attractive. The same thing happens when you fight with your partner and you want to fill the void with a bucket of ice cream, liters of beer or a pair of new shoes. The void won't be filled up and then you will also have an additional void in your finances, or a stomach ache!

The process by which human beings desire things and we develop energy to achieve them is one of the most important and special things that make us unique on this planet. Almost all the books on success written in the United States make reference to the fact that the first thing needed to achieve success is to have a dream. The famous "American dream", which sounds corny to some, is in fact the biological bases for achieving the necessary energy to progress in life. Let me explain it to you on a very basic hormonal level. Human beings are driven by different hormones that exist to help us in different instances of life. We will talk about two of them. These wonderful hormones that we were gifted with, exist in each of us, among many others and therefore, we are all equal in terms of having the inside chemistry needed in order to succeed.

One of them is dopamine, the hormone of achievement, reward and one of the hormones in charge of happiness. It is the hormone of satisfaction after the accomplishment of a task. When thousands of years ago, men hunted in packs, we arrived to town with food, maybe dragging a mammoth and we were greeted like heroes by all. Since then, when we achieve something, what happens at a chemical level is that our brain is flooded with dopamine and the release of this powerful neurotransmitter gives us immense pleasure. The sensations are so strong that we are willing to risk our lives in order to feel the rush that it produces, and in large, thanks to it, the human being would go out hunting again. This way the survival of our species was ensured.

When a person wants something, whatever it is, a new cell phone, a car, a house or recognition, on a biological level, internally, a process takes place that culminates when the person achieves what they had proposed; At that moment dopamine is released, the reward hormone. All the desire, the energy, the strength and motivation to obtain it, are triggered by the desire to feel that pleasure produced after the release of dopamine in the body.

We can say then, that it's natural for us to desire improvements in our lives and feel highly motivated to achieve them. Our own biology supports this claim, and that means that when you use deferred gratification, you are using all the power of your own nature.

However, with bank loans and the microwave mentality with which we want everything now, human beings themselves are sabotaging all our natural and biological power. Let's do a simple example: Imagine you want a new cell phone, the latest phone from your favorite brand. It's about $1,300 and you decide to make it your goal to buy it. "When I achieve such result in my entrepreneurship or obtain a certain thing, I'll give myself that phone as a reward." This works with any prize and in any scale. For example, you could say "when I get three properties generating an income of $2,000 a month, I'll buy that new car that I love." So far so good. To fuel your dream and turn it into what success books call "A burning desire", you go to look at your cell phone or do a test drive of the car that you want. You see it, you smell it, and you feel it. You listen to the engine to increase the desire and energy that the dream produces. Up to that moment, everything is fantastic. Every time, you're more committed to the goal you've set in order to enjoy your reward. The problem is, when the seller arrives and tells you: "if you like it, just for today we have an amazing offer, you can take it for % less. In addition, we will finance it, and the monthly payments would be left at just... ", fill in the spaces yourself; $30 a month on the phone? $400 a month for the car? If you fall for the trap, you'll do something fatal ... you'll sabotage your hormones and damage the process by which you were going to have all the energy and motivation to achieve what you had proposed. There'll no longer be any dopamine left, since it is produced as a result of making an effort and achieving something.

Dopamine is not released by possessing objects. It's released when those objects are the reward for a job well done which required effort. Without the effort, there is no dopamine. That's why people buy things on credit and feel no lasting satisfaction from them. The natural process of setting goals to improve our lives and feeling the energy to achieve them is broken down by your own self every time you agree to give yourself an award without having won it. We then have a lot of people out there saying that they don't know why they aren't motivated. They say things like "I don't think I know what my dream is" and the only truth is that they themselves sabotaged their biology, stealing their own source of energy and then falling into apathy.

Many young people today suffer from this, because their parents have not taught them to set goals and work for them, but instead have flooded them with material things in exchange for no effort. The reality is that many parents today have an immense feeling of guilt, most times for not having enough time to spend with their family and with their children. They try to fill that void of time and appease the guilt, by giving them gifts and providing them with experiences that only tend to maintain the distance between parents and children, by not doing them together. What young people's brains are registering is that they don't have to strive to achieve anything and that everything comes to them for free or worse, through emotional blackmail. Young people then, unconsciously, look for that dopamine in other sources, for example, in drugs such as cocaine that promote the accumulation of dopamine.

I once heard that at a symposium on drug addiction, a great businessman said, in a short speech, before some of the most influential politicians in the United States, that the drug problem lies on the fact that the parents of these drug addicted children didn't have dreams and therefore hadn't taught their children to have dreams. If we take into context the need to generate dopamine, these words take on a lot of truth.

There is a second guest in this common process of buying ourselves everything immediately and on credit; it's the second hormone that we will talk about: cortisol, the stress hormone, which is triggered in our body because of bad debts, by generating concern and a feeling of risk. Having high levels of cortisol has effects on the metabolism of fats, carbohydrates and proteins and can cause a rise in blood sugar, resulting in an increased risk of Type 2 Diabetes. Cortisol also alters the functions of inflammatory levels in the body, blood pressure, sleep cycle, memory and concentration. Maintaining high levels of cortisol in the body, for long periods of time, due to chronic stress, is equivalent for our brain to experience that we are in permanent risk of survival and this causes our whole organism to wear out, it weakens the immune system and opens the door to serious illness. As if that were not enough, it makes us intolerable to the people around us, also affecting our relationships and quality of life.

Delayed gratification is then a healthy, natural and recommended practice for human beings. If we add the information on compound interest to it, the phrase by R. Kiyosaki with which we opened this sub chapter, makes a lot more sense, because if we buy the luxuries at the beginning, we will be wasting valuable seeds that could bring us millions in the future. Like this, we can understand that it's much more expensive to buy now than later and that it's smart to acquire our luxuries with the cashflows produced by our assets and returns from the investments we make, instead of paying for them with the sweat of our hard work. To do the opposite would be as if you wanted to eat the seeds before planting them, instead of waiting for the harvest when you will have lots of seeds to do whatever you want with.

Is it easy to put these two principles into practice? No. But it's worth it. Anything worth doing is worth doing wrong until you get it right. If you were offered an extra $100,000 a year to at-

FINANCIAL DETOX

tend to the German clients of the company you work for and that meant you had to learn German, how would you speak it at first? You would be a disaster, you would feel ashamed, it would seem very difficult. However, if you persist, you will end up speaking it quite well and in addition to the $100,000 extra a year, you will be proud of having achieved it. The same thing happens with saving and with these 2 principles I taught you. It will take effort, but it's worth it.

> **Anything worth doing, is worth doing wrong, until you get it right.**

If starting with 10% seems like a lot to you, start with less, but start. You decide with how much, but start today. The moment you start saving, whatever percentage it may be, you get this new belief: "I am abundant, I earn more than I spend and I can save, so I have seeds to invest and become rich", as opposed to "I can't", that ends your aspirations forever.

Of course, if you are going to save less than 10%, commit to the fact that when you increase your income you will complete that 10%. Let's do an example. Let's say you earned $2,000 today and decided you want to start with 5% because you can't imagine starting with more than that. That means you will save $100. Then one day you raise your income thanks to the advice given to you in this book or because your salary increased and now you earn $2,200. At that moment, according to the commitment you made, you will save 10%, that is, $220 per month. Since you already saved $100 before, the new amount implies a saving of an additional $120, but your income increased by $200. Even doing so, you still have enough to spend a little more per month on whatever you want, but you fully meet your goal of 10%.

59

If you learn to do this with each increase in your income, you will see how in a matter of time, you can save 20%, 40% or 50% of your income, accelerating the speed with which you achieve your financial freedom. Committing to saving with your future income is something that anyone believes they can do and if you decide to do it now, then you will have no problem executing it.

The most important thing is that starting today you begin with the habit, everything else you can adjust along the way, the amount you save, the interest you obtain for the type of investment you make and the frequency with which you contribute to your investment funds. They can improve over time, but start today and a new world will open up for you, believe me, you want to live in this new world and you can do it. Just get started already!

@COACH_FINANCIERO, WHAT DO I DO? ¿PAY OFF DEBTS OR START SAVING?

We could say that this is one of the questions we receive most frequently. When we elevate financial intelligence to the point where we already believe we are capable of producing that glorious monthly cashflow, we begin to feel empowered. So we review our possibilities and the logical question is now what do I do? Do I pay off debts or do I start saving?

It's a difficult question to answer because there isn't a single answer. It depends on each person's personal financial situation, their level of discipline and their financial intelligence. It also has to do with the level of emotional intelligence that a person has. It has to do with the experience you have as an investor and the ability to achieve good returns on capital at a low risk.

The professional and logical answer is very simple, make a comparison between the interests you are paying for those debts vs. the interest you can get on an investment and put your money where there is greater interest. If, for example, you have a loan in which you pay 10% annual interest and you only get investments in which they give you 5%; then pay off the debt first without hesitation. On the other hand, if you can obtain returns of 18% and your debt is a 30-year mortgage that charges you 4% or the debt of a car that charges you 7%, we would tell you, it's better if you invest!

Over time, we have perceived that this answer has many nuances. For example, what happens if you don't know how to invest and you lose money? You would be left with debt and without money. What if you are in a situation of financial risk and you can lose your job and your only source of income in the short term? Then you better make a provision fund. Do you already have a contingency fund? Are you single or do you have a partner? Does your partner also make money? Do you have children? Are you the type of person that's good at facing risky emotional tolerance or do you drown in a glass of water when it comes to thinking about risky investments? Do I make myself clear in what I'm trying to tell you? Every situation and every person in every situation makes the answer to the question change.

In this chapter, we are going to address this question assuming that the person asking us the question is an ordinary person, with no investment experience, almost nothing or very little in their savings, and with considerable bad debt that takes away a good part of their income each month, between payments, interest and associated expenses. In addition, we will assume that these debts and payments cause, as in almost all people and families, anxiety and problems, both health wise and in their relationships.

Maintaining high levels of stress in the body and mind for a long period of time is very complicated because it can cause physical and mental illnesses. Fear (stress) has a vital function of preserving life in survival mode. It is essential in life-threatening situations and is an activator of necessary bodily functions. When we lived in caves, in the ice age, and giant mammals with immense fangs chased us, stress was appreciated because it made us have a lot of energy in our arms and legs, we could run faster than ever, climb trees or defend ourselves with skill.

Animals in the jungle continue to survive thanks to this type of stress, and in dangerous situations they generate cortisol to survive the different attacks they face in nature. Once they overcome the specific situation of danger, the stress goes away and normality returns. Free roaming wild animals don't suffer then from the terrible consequences of this prolonged and accumulated stress.

Today's human being is not concerned with preserving life in the sense of surviving predator attacks, but rather spends countless hours of the day and night stressed out by their problems, in many cases financial and in most cases, problems arising from debts. We could extend ourselves on this subject, but it's not the objective of this book. What is important to understand is that for the vast majority, solving their debts would bring a considerable increase in their quality of life. Therefore, emotional conditions must be assessed when evaluating whether to pay off debts or even better, save and invest.

Without taking into account each person's particular situations, which as I told you, can make this answer vary substantially, we would give an ordinary person the following formula:

1) Create a *freedom cashflow* (earn more than you spend). You will get this cashflow by following the advice in this book, reducing your expenses and increasing your income. You will understand this concept better in the chapter on *freedom cashflow* to kill off bad debts.

2) Pay off the abusive debts that you have in default or that are charging you high interest (more than 1.2% per month or 14% per year).

3) Build a financial cushion equal to 3-6 or 12 months of expenses, depending on the stability of your income.

4) Continue paying off debts and eliminate all those that are above 5% per year.

5) Keep eliminating your other low-interest debts (such as the mortgage), but allocate part of your cashflow to saving and investing and start learning about returns and investment options in which you find returns greater than what you pay on these low credits cost; Start small and from there go step by step.

6) Any bonus or prize that you receive that isn't part of your normal income; allocate it according to this list to cover 1 to 5.

7) Never stop learning, keep investing and researching and find the investment formula in the area that you like the most and that is aligned with your values; be it financial products such as the stock market, business or real estate.

When you get out of those harmful bad debts that not only

affect your income but your self-esteem, you will see a great increase in your confidence and self-esteem. You will be more willing to tolerate risk and doors will open up for you that you didn't know of before, because all your energy was going into paying off those debts instead of dedicating it to prosper. In the next chapters you will discover the massive formula to eliminate bad debts forever.

#STOP_FINANCIAL_
BULLYING

At these times, it's very common to talk about bullying. The truth is that now the word is trending and the damage it does to children has been made aware, although it has always existed and not only among young people, but in all ages and even industries, politics, jobs, etc. Now we will refer to one of the strongest and most prolonged bullying to which people are subjected to and it's of the financial type.

Bullying is the harassment that a person has been a victim of by someone who has power over them. This power can be physical, as it happens with children; however, in most cases the strongest consequence occurs on a psychological level and remains even when the bullying has ended. For bullying to be effective, there must be persistency of that condition. That is, if it's only a one time situation, it's not bullying, it is an altercation. The bully or harasser tends to constantly exert pressure on his/her victim in various ways, reminding them that they are power-less under him/her and striking their self-esteem. It's common for him/her to make practical jokes, use derogatory and hu-miliating nicknames, and do it on a regular basis to keep that pressure on. The bully imparts many doses of fear, uses social pressure by humiliating the person in front of others and only on some occasions reaches physical aggression that could com-promise their own integrity. The less need to use actual force, the more successful they become as a harasser.

A victim of bullying, since they're constantly thinking about the harassment, suffers from a persecution that never ends, impairing not only their mental capacity, but also draining their energy in the worry and negative projection that bullying causes them. They are losing their life, for life is energy. A child may spend a lot of time figuring out how to avoid encounter-ing his/her bullies and then starts looking for excuses skipping class; constantly thinking of hiding or running away. In extreme cases, as has become common in the United States, even mas-sacres have been committed by victims of bullying.

Perhaps the most dangerous thing about bullying is that in the short term it's very effective. That's why we see more and more presidents of countries and company directors use bullying in their day-to-day lives. This way, they carry out ex-treme policies that mistreat a lot and prioritize short-term profitability over long term. Obviously, the largest capitals we have are human beings, and through these policies harm others, undermining their trust and losing their loyalty, which are vital values for long-term business and commercial relationships. Those benefits that immediate bullying brings are too dan-gerous, since they could cost these politicians and corporate executives their teams, their clients and even their own com-pany or division of a country.

The financial system is a master in the practice of bullying and works as a team with other very powerful industries, such as the press, consumer industry and the automotive industry. Publicity in part, is responsible for bombarding you with advertisements of all the things you "should have" in order for your life to be perfect. They make you believe in your subconscious mind that you will achieve complete happiness by buying that phone, that car, that property or if you go on vacation. And then banks and finance companies enter the scene, which are there to offer you a loan that will make it possible. Become aware for one week of how many times you are bombarded to buy something and in how many different ways, from TV commercials, billboards, ads when browsing the web, posts on your social media, flyers in your mailbox, commercials when watching videos on YouTube, etc. Everything is part of what we have called **"financial bullying"** with the sole purpose of having you give them your money, your power, your energy, and therefore your life. Offers are also raining down on you to get that Visa credit card and as you already know … "for everything else, there is MasterCard." They show you your dream car and at the bottom a small fee that you have to pay every month. They aren't showing you that in order to achieve that fee you would have to do a down payment first of almost half the value of the vehicle and the other half when finalizing. You go on your bank's website and they show you offers on financial products that seem like free money and you'd be a fool if you didn't take it. Not to mention the calls they make promoting banking products, mortgages, consumer loans and other cards, even for commercial establishments.

They exhaust you before starting any transaction, because the bombardment happens before you buy something or take one of their products. Then comes the harassment of receiving the collection bills at home, the saturation of your email inbox with banking communications and now that we have apps, individual notifications. This is how traditional financial bullying works. In addition, take notice of all the products that they flood you with, without even having asked for them? Like insurance policies that you don't need or credit cards you don't want?

I remember one time my sister-in-law told us that they were suddenly called to collect a debt that they hadn't paid and that they had never acquired. My brother-in-law is a doctor and it turns out that one day when he was working in his office, they called him to offer him a credit card. He told them that at the moment he couldn't answer them and they asked him if he was at least interested. At the end of the call, he said yes, but that he couldn't speak at the moment and that they would talk later. Well, it turns out that they took that "yes" as enough to issue the card and start charging them a monthly fee. Upon finding out, the bank replied that any "yes" was enough. Laws, as sad as it may be, many times protect and favor financial bullying, so you have to be very careful and the best thing is to say decisively: **I AM NOT INTERESTED, REMOVE ME FROM THE DATABASE, YOU ARE VIOLATING MY PRIVACY.**

Now ... what happens if you're late on payments? Well then, that's where professional harassment begins, threats for late payments, enforcement of punishments such as interest for delayed payments, threats from lawyers, and threats to pursue your assets and those of your co-debtors, if that's the case. It is followed by the calls to collect and nowadays they also cede your obligations to third parties, who begin to call you and harass you as well, something you don't remember ever authorizing. Finally, the real threat: a legal process that carries out a lot of expenses for you, having to hire a lawyer for yourself and having to pay for theirs, the commissions of the intermediaries and everything else, just to end up losing the property you had bought.

Apart from this, you receive utility bills such as electricity, water, gas, cable TV, internet, cell phones, content subscriptions, and platforms and websites that charge you for their use.

Let's add the taxes, income tax, automobile circulation tax, property taxes, if you are a merchant, the sales tax, trade tax, and others. In short ... everything that needs to be paid for so that the tax office doesn't go after you. Every day in the press and on television news, there are news that intimidates all those who may not comply with the payment of taxes, and they repeat how they can even end up in jail and that basically, their life is over.

You can say that it's normal and logical that they charge you, and it is something that I can't argue with, but think for a moment the effect that all this has on your subconscious and the load of stress that it brings to your life. Do you realize the similarities it has with the bullying that goes on in schools? You are a psychological prey to the constant abuse of power. Most people feel helpless and weak in the face of this pressure from financial institutions and just want to get out of the trouble and be left alone.

Many are willing to give up their idea of a better life and the start up of a company because of the fear that they've endured after so much financial bullying. We've come across atrocious thinking patterns. One of the most terrifying is, "why should I start up something if the estate will just keep everything?" If they affirm this way of thinking, they could also ask themselves, "Why stay alive if I am going to die?" They are giving up on creating the life they could have and canceling the race before it even starts. All because the financial bullying that they've experienced in their lives has made them so traumatized that they prefer to withdraw from the race before even trying.

A victim of financial bullying also spends their time projecting negative scenarios about future finances, in a panic of losing their home, source of income, freedom, the love of their family and their health. In the most extreme cases, we see how some flee or even end up taking their own life, just as a child would who can't find a way to escape school because their life is hell as a result of bullying.

Well, this chapter is about saying **NO MORE!** I will not be a prey to bullying. I will impose my conditions because it is my money and I can decide. I have the power in this post-industrial era as a Consumer and whoever doesn't like it can go where we already know! The first great *financial detox* that we propose will be this financial bullying detox. Now that we're aware that we're victims of bullying, we have a huge advantage, we're adults and we have the ability to stop it and never fall into it again.

A couple of years ago, I saw how a strange charge for a small amount began to appear on my credit card bill every month, and all it had was an identity code that was SEG ####, where #### was a 4 digit number. When I called the bank to ask what it was, they told me that it was an insurance that I had contracted. Upon finding out what type of insurance it was, they told me it was for protection against theft at ATMs when withdrawing money. At that time I was living outside of that country, so I told them that I hadn't requested it because I didn't have the need to withdraw money at an ATM. They told me that I should file a complaint because the system stated that I had accepted that insurance. I asked them what proof they had that I had accepted it, and they told me that there had to be a recording since it was verified in the system that they had called my phone to confirm the acceptance of the insurance. My phone had been disconnected for months, since I already lived in another country.

The first thing I did was to express how upset I was and the injustice committed on my social media, in which we have tens of thousands of followers. I pointed them out in the comments and said there was no right for this happening. Immediately, we began to receive comments from people who had something similar happen to them and expressed their support and disagreement with the banks' behavior.

They contacted me shortly after that through my social media, apologizing for everything and asking me for more information about the case. The speed with which they respond on social media is impressive. A negative post can cost them thousands of customers, as it happened with a musician who a few years ago, posted a video in which his guitar had been broken at an airline due to the mistreatment while handling his luggage. That event was an economic disaster for the airline, it even affected the value of its stock in the stock market, it marked an era in which, we as customers have power through social media and we can massively express our disagreement in a way never before contemplated.

I then proceeded to write to the bank office where I have my personal and business accounts and also wrote directly to the director of that office. I told him I wanted to start an investigation for fraud and identity theft. I explained how they were charging me for an insurance that I had not requested and how they told me that they had a recording on a date in which I wasn't even in the country, where I had accepted the monthly charges. I sent out a copy of my passport exit stamps from the country proving that it was impossible for me to have received such a call. I asked them for brevity in the investigation and access to the recording because my lawyer would file a criminal complaint in this regard, since I was the victim of impersonation and fraud. In less than 20 minutes, I received a call from the office manager apologizing and saying that there must have been a misunderstanding. He told me that they had already reversed the charges and as compensation, they would also cancel fixed charges from the card. I told him that was fine, but that I was still concerned about my safety and wanted to proceed with the investigation. He told me he would discuss it with the area in charge. Days later, I received another call in which it was explained to me that it had been due to an internal error, and that as it was evident, I hadn't been in the country on those days when they supposedly had called me.

I immediately thought of the number of people who, unlike me, continue paying this hidden charge month after month, without being aware of it and the millions that the banks are awarded at the expense of dupes who don't use their power and let themselves be bullied. Some out of carelessness, since most don't even review their bank statements, others because of laziness to claim and others because they believe that there's nothing to do in the face of these banking and business titans. Trust me, they're like David and Goliath, you can make them fall with a stone and slingshot; in these times, social media is our our slingshot and posts are our stones, and it can make any giant kneel down.

Dear reader, the next step is to make a plan to communicate to each of those who bully us that their days of abuse of power have come to an end and that we are not going to put up with it any longer. In the future, we will ask them for options to reduce debt, and we will be the ones who propose a payment plan that adjusts to our financial plan; this way, getting out of bad debts, saving and investing, and building the free and solid future that we deserve.

Remember that financial institutions, like all others, compete with each other and spend huge budgets on marketing and advertising to get and retain their customers. Imagine that after having invested all that money in having you as a client, you pick up the phone, call them and tell them "I'm leaving you for someone else." Well that's what you're going to do!

PART TWO

TAKE CONTROL

LOWER EXPENSES: THE MAGIC OF CREATING A POSITIVE CASHFLOW NOW!

By Catalina Cortés

W e can all create a new monthly positive cashflow starting today if we learn to adjust certain or better, all the expenses in our house. It's a magical process, not suitable for lazy people. You're going to have to make calls, estimates and movements that will require time and attention, but which, like magic, will free your money; which will become a spectacular positive cashflow that will start the wave of freedom or what we'll later call "the freedom cashflow".

And how is this done? I'm going to explain it to you in detail, but first I need you to understand that this is a process that will require you to have discipline and patience. Most people don't do it because they feel like it's going to be too much work, but I hope you do and understand that it's worth it. In this life, we make all our decisions for two reasons, to avoid pain or to seek pleasure. So, I hope you understand that this exercise will help you reduce the pain in your life, since you'll be spending less and having less worries, but it will also increase your pleasure enormously in the future with the use of that cashflow.

The economy of a house is made up of many micro expenses. These micro expenses added up become a large sum of money. Don't underestimate lowering one of those expenses down to 10 or 20 dollars. Everything adds up. And in the end, it's those little adjustments that are going to do the magic. Many people say: "but do all that just to save 10 a month? What nonsense!" This book is designed so that those 10 are added to another 20, 50 on the other hand and 500 or 1000 from another strategy; don't belittle them. Remember that with the cost of a cup of coffee a day you can become a millionaire, as we saw in the chapter on compound interest. Everything adds up, so watch the big screen and don't get caught up in the petty details. This is a part of our *financial detox*, and as little as it may seem, it's about removing from our personal financial system everything that intoxicates us so that we can free up space to plant the new seeds of prosperity.

We have a gift for you!

In this book, we don't go into detail in teaching you how to make a budget, because we know that there are many books and videos on the internet that can help you with that. In the following QR code you can download a format to help you make your own budget; this format will also help you to get your P&L (Profit and Loss) status and to make an analysis of income vs. expenses.

So let's get to work! First you need to create a list as complete as possible of all your expenses, the basics, the variables, the weekly, monthly, quarterly, semi-annual, and annual; all of them. Most budgets fail to ignore micro-expenses thinking they're insignificant, but when added together, they can put a dent in your finances. I am going to divide them to create several positive cashflows in different categories of expenses:

- Basic services: water, electricity, natural gas, cell phone, internet, television, subscription services.

- Home expenses: mortgage, taxes, administration or community expenses.

- Food: market.

- Insurance: health, home, car, professional, life insurance, pets.

- Education: school, university, tutors, sports.

- Entertainment: dinner dates, getaways, vacations.

- Clothing: clothes, uniforms.

- Transportation. (Parking, Valet, Gasoline, shop, etc.)

Basic Services:

Water

Although in most countries there are no companies that compete to provide this service, there are things that you can implement to use less water in your home and lower the bill just a bit, such as:

- Use water savers in your faucet and shower. They can save you between 18% and 47% of water.

- Use a cup when brushing your teeth.

- Use the dishwasher by filling it to its maximum capacity, you can save a significant percentage of water and it will free up time.

- Use concentrated dish soaps that are easily diluted in water. That way you can use the short cycle of your washer machine that rinses only 1 time, instead of 2 like the normal cycle.

- Keep your faucets, sinks, showers and toilets in good condition so they don't leak.

Electricity

In countries like USA and Spain there are different companies that provide electricity service, so you can call and have an estimate from at least 3 different companies and see what each one offers. I always lean towards those that produce their electricity in a clean (ecological) way.

These companies offer time slots where electricity is cheaper, so that you can take advantage of those hours and use the appliances that consume the most during that time, such as the dishwasher, the dryer, the washer machine, the water heater. The savings are huge! You just need to schedule yourself to use these devices during those times and you will have a positive cashflow of 20 or 30 dollars per month.

If this competency doesn't exist in your country, it's best to look for timers for some appliances. For example, we use one for the water filter because we know that we don't need purified water between certain hours of the night and early in the morning, so why have the appliance turned on consuming electricity? Same goes for the water heater. You can do the same with your home Wi-Fi and in fact, doctors recommend it to reduce the waves and magnetism in your home. If you don't do it for the savings, do it for your health! You can also choose natural gas appliances, which are cheaper, and you can opt for energy-efficient technologies as well.

Recently at a seminar in the USA a couple taught me that by changing the light bulbs for Led lights, they had generated a savings of up to 50 dollars on their bill. Sure, they're more expensive to buy, but they last much longer and their efficiency compared to the traditional ones is superior, almost 90% more; and since what we want is to free up a monthly cashflow, it applies 100 percent.

Natural gas

If you have a natural gas connection in your home, you already have a great advantage. Gas appliances have very high efficiency and consume little.

Landline and cell phone service

The first thing I want you to think about is that having a landline at home is a waste of resources. Today, hardly anyone uses a landline; so you can cut it out of your expenses. We already know that your internet company wants to sell you one at all costs and includes it in the packages, but you know what? That's Financial Bullying, don't allow it! Remember: #STOP_financial_bullying. In phone companies, there's a lot of competition and that's in favor of us customers. Understand that the game here is, that you as a customer have the power and you must use it. If we emphasize something in our face-to-face seminars, it's on this point: Empowering the consumer. You have the power to decide and you must demand it. The era of big monopolies is over, even if it's in these areas. Now the competition gives you the advantage. Learn to use it.

Once a year, Fer and I re-budget all of our services. We look for which company gives us the best advantages, at the lowest cost. We list 5 companies on average, including the one we're already in. We do it with a lot of attitude, that's the key. You need to empower yourself and call to see what they can offer you and how they can improve your service.

Do something as simple as putting on your social media, "how much do you pay for your cell phone plan?" Ask your acquaintances if any of them pay less. You will see what happens, many new options will appear. With those figures you can call those companies and see what they can offer you.

Cable Television

Although you can do the same exercise as with your cell phone, the real question is: Do I really need a cable television service? The truth is that with Smart TV, Netflix, Amazon prime and/or YouTube, or with those specific sports that you like, you don't need much more. You never watch most of the channels anyway! Plus, without cable TV, you'll stop wasting so much time flipping through channels, and it can be an incentive to read more and learn about more interesting topics.

Subscription services

In the era of apps, payment channels, online magazines, etc., most of us have between 3 and 5 monthly or annual subscriptions that we don't use. Many times we don't even remember we have them and since they have a "low" cost on the credit card bill, we don't even realize that we are still paying for them. It's time to Detox from all those small charges and start verifying which of them are really essential or even desired. You can just cancel the others immediately!

Insurance policies

Here the key is to really know what insurance you need and which ones are not essential at this stage of your life. It is normal now a days to have insurance for everything, but do you really need that many? Make a list of all the insurances you have and analyze them to see which ones you need. There are countries in which, due to safety problems, having their cell phone insured is important, while in others it isn't. Life insurance is important for a person with a family, while a young single person doesn't really need it in most cases.

Health insurance can be important depending on your country; there are places with an excellent public health service, while in others it's very basic. When you have decided if it's necessary, you can start to estimate the service cost of the different companies. Do you go to the doctor often? There are some companies where you pay a small fee for the medical appointment, and there are others where you don't; some cover you abroad, or have greater coverage throughout the country. These elements are the variables that determine the price. Think about, how often do you travel to other cities? Do you travel abroad frequently? I have acquaintances that pay a very expensive travel insurance and they never leave the city.

After this analysis and knowing exactly what type of service you need, now you can make price comparisons and decide on the one that best suits your real needs. Remember to do it with 3 to 5 companies, no less.

Home insurance: We have always had our properties insured; it's something that gives us peace of mind. There's a lot of variety in this area. They cover you from structural damage, theft, to changing the silicone in the bathtub. Decide what type of insurance you need and proceed to make the price comparison with the companies; you already know how it is.

Be careful with the insurances that banks require you to have for mortgages. In most cases, after a year you could have that same insurance with any external company and surely get a better price. Find out. In addition, ask them to explain each of those insurances that they require you to have. How long are they for? What do they cover? Could you have it with a different entity from theirs?

When you travel, some credit cards offer you medical insurance abroad or car rental. It's interesting to know what they offer you and with what requirements. Most of the Black, Platinum or Premium cards give you these insurances for free as well as VIP lounges in different airports around the world. If you are a person who travels a lot, those things are appreciated.

Entertainment

The point here is to plan ahead. If you want a trip, plan it in advance, you'll find better deals on tickets, hotels and excursions that way. Don't be lazy, buy your own the tickets; if you go to a travel agency in most cases it'll be more expensive. Just enter in your search engine and look up online tickets, you'll find many. We always estimate costs through airline portals and websites. Sometimes it's better to buy directly from the airline and sometimes through ticket search engines. You can also put a price reduction alert and the system will send you a notification when there are sales to your chosen destinations.

You can get tour guides in the cities you're going to visit, look for accommodation or review portals. We are not "tour guide" travelers; for us, buying tours is like paying someone to be your boss on vacation. I remember when we traveled to China for almost a month with some friends. Since we like to enjoy each place at our own pace, we made a direct contact on the internet with a young guide who had very good comments, we spoke with him through chat and we made the visits with his team in the different cities. It was a spectacular trip. We got to know the sites with local guides from each city, we learned a lot about their culture and we went at our own rythm. We paid less than half of what other friends who took tours paid. We have done the same in Morocco, Turkey, Jordan and most of the 51 countries that we have visited to this today.

Use portals that offer discounts on restaurants, spa experiences, or getaways; you'll be surprised on how much you can do for less. There are also gyms, yoga classes, beauty treatments, hairdressing, nail salons and other activities that are advertised there, with discounts of up to 80%.

Shopping

Shopping is a pleasure that I enjoy. I have to accept it, like most women and a growing number of men. I suggest you do it during the sales season and take a shopping list. In image consulting, I learned that most of the things we buy out of emotion, we hardly ever use. Many are things that looked nice in the store, but that don't go with your style, or with your wardrobe.

I always carry a list of things that I need or that can be a good purchase option. I usually plan two shopping trips a year, during the sales season or at the Outlets. I'm not really interested in buying things from last season.

When we go to buy big things, like furniture or technology, we compare many online stores and then we wait a few days before buying. We wonder, do we really need it? If after five days you think you do, then choose the best offer. Although Fer is a fan of technology, he always waits a bit after the releases to see what real improvements they bring and if it's worth it.

At this point emotional intelligence is the most important thing. Avoid getting carried away by your biological instincts to buy just for buying. Don't buy things to impress your friends either, they don't care. We see people making large purchases all the time, like expensive vehicles, and they're people who have no investment in rentals or worse, they take on bad debt to buy those things!

Transportation

For all those who live outside of the USA, it is absolutely shocking to see how much people spend in valet parking. It is common for people to give up $10-$20 dollars every time they go to a hotel, restaurant or mall. It can add up to valuable cashflow that you are letting go every week. Also, compare car services and memberships you have. Look for alternatives. Find a cashflow conscious friend and carpool for example. This is something you need to look into.

By applying yourself to do what I have taught you in this chapter, with dedication and determination, I can guarantee that you will be able to free up treasured dollars per month that, combined with everything else you are learning, will add to your freedom cashflow with which we will build your financial freedom. I emphasize that you don't let yourself be taken over by laziness and also that it's not just a onetime thing. Repeating this work year after year is invaluable; since service providers renew their offers and tend to favor new customers over old ones, whom they see as long-term dairy cows for which no big gestures are required because they're already used to their service. You are different, you're here to experience only the best and you're going to make it clear to them that, to retain you they will have to give you the VIP treatment.

DEBT RESTRUCTURING, REFINANCE UNDER YOUR OWN TERMS.

In their commercial war, financial institutions seek not only to attract new clients, but also to steal their competitors' clients. They do so by offering them better conditions. As well as TV and telephone companies, financial companies offer to absorb the credits of others, subrogate mortgages, take out new cards in which your previous debts are consolidated or offer you investment credits that will allow you to pay off all your other debts and be left with just that debt but with better conditions in terms of interest, fees and delivery terms.

This will free you hundreds of dollars in cashflow, allowing you to redirect them towards the same payment of those debts. All this adds up significantly in our *financial detox*, detoxifying ourselves from expensive interest and charges that your sick finances may have.

I will give you a personal example of the brutal impact this has on your cashflow. A couple of years ago, we bought some investment properties. As we were not tax residents at that time in Spain, the country where we made this investment, we had difficulty finding loans. A bank offered us a loan in which the terms were good, except that the delivery term in which we had to pay was only 10 years. This being the case, the monthly fee was very high (€2,600) and what we received for rent didn't even cover the amount (€2,500), excluding insurance plus other expenses. Having no better alternative at that time and not wanting to pay it in cash, we decided to take it because we were buying those properties at a very good price. Later in the chapter where we talk about real estate investments, we'll tell you how to do good deals in that industry, but for now the important thing is to see how loans operate.

A year later, we arrived with the statements, certificates and rental contracts, which showed how these properties were being managed correctly and were constantly producing money in that country month after month. In addition, we certified other incomes in that country as a result of our business work and our *money-making machine*. We asked the bank to reconsider the conditions and we provided the documentation. Days later they answered that it wasn't possible; the commercial agent who attended us told us that the bank knew we could pay that fee, so why would they lower it.

Instantly, with Cata, we said to ourselves: "Oh yeah? Well, you'll see me leave with someone else!" and we started knocking on doors at different banks. Through referrals, we arrived at one that offered to extend the delivery term from 10 to 25 years, keep the terms; but as the properties had also raised their value in that period of time and now the property appraisal was much higher, they offered to give us 25% more of the money we owed at the time so that we could allocate it to whatever we wanted. This meant we could extend the mortgage. Results in our cashflow? On the one hand, the installments were lowered to half, leaving us now with a beautiful profit and liberating a cashflow of more than €1,300 per month. On the other hand, with the 25% extra they gave us, we could buy another property that left us an additional €500. In practical terms, the exercise freed us €1,800 per month, for the simple act of not conforming and insisting until we got the terms that worked for us.

Maybe you've been paying your mortgage for many years, maybe the value of the property has risen, maybe inflation is different than it was when you took out the loan, maybe the bank changed its policies, and maybe there are new competitors in the market that offer better terms. Perhaps it was you who changed and now you're much more attractive to the financial sector that's willing to lend you money on better terms; because in their analysis you are much more reliable and represent less risk. It may also be that when you took out the loan, an interest of 5% per year was normal and now it's around 2.5%; that means that you have a high probability of lowering the interest you are paying by half. Can you imagine? That's half the cost. Perhaps there's a bank or an office that hasn't met its goals and the managers are desperate to meet them in anyway they can. I don't know! What I do know is that if you look, you will find!

Subrogation, novation, debt absorption, all are ways of naming something that means the same to you: improving your cashflow. Sometimes entities, in order to not lose customers, change the terms of their own mortgage, but don't expect them to call informing you of this. When you do this process, make sure you go to at least three banks in addition to yours. Ask to speak to the office manager and meet him. The world of banking and credit is very subjective. The same bank in different branches offers loans under different conditions and many times, the difference depends on whether or not you have a relationship with the director of the branch. On the other hand, we know people who haven't been given a financial product in the office they've been loyal to all their life, such as a "renting" in real estate, but when asking at an office in another city from the same bank, by phone or being recommended by someone else who had already done that figure of renting, they gave it to them.

Part of the helplessness that we humans feel about banks, is that we believe that they use a unique and inflexible method alien to human emotions and free from any influence that we may exert. This is not the case in practice. Banks have a risk office that analyzes the documents you attach when studying your credit; but ultimately, it's a human being who makes the decision, as in everything. If you present yourself in front of directors of bank offices, show them professionalism and a trustworthy image and tell them about your desire to transfer your financial products to that new bank. You will increase, by a higher percentage, your chances of getting better terms.

At school and at university they rate us with letters or numbers. In my case it was over 10 in school and then over 5 at university. There are other educational institutions where they do it with letters such as A, B, C and D for deficient. At banks we also have our own scoring sheet. The difference is that when we are adults, school or university grades don't matter. Banks could care less. Can you imagine presenting yourself to a bank manager and saying: "I want to buy an investment property and I need a mortgage, here are my grades from college, 4.5 in Geography, 4 in Mathematics and a 5 in Biology." I think the bank clerk will burst out laughing, don't you agree?

What they'll look at, are your financial statements which are two: your annual results (P&L for profit and loss) that talks about how much you earn and how much you spend, and your balance or equity (what you have minus what you owe). The bank will rate you with a number that tells them how much risk implies in loaning you the money and also what they can get their hands on in case you don't pay.

We have another gift for you!

If you follow this QR code, you will be able to download a format to help you get your balance. You can make a list of your assets and liabilities and thus analyze your assets and what you will present to the bank.

Depending on that, they will decide first whether or not to lend you money, and second, on what terms. Depending on this, will be the interest they lend you at (the higher the risk you represent, the higher the interest on the loan), the time period for which they will lend you for (which depends on your age and the strength that your activity projects economically), the amount that they will lend you (according to the current value of the home in the appraisal) which can range from 100% of the credit you bring and even offer you more money, for example 25% more, like I said happened to us, because the property had gone up in price.

Once you establish contact with three banks in addition to yours, you should make a folder of documents that can prove your financial strength so as to be attractive to the bank. Keep in mind the following, banks will analyze several things: the stability of your income, your assets, your cashflow and your other debts. They will study something called your debt capacity, which means that they will look at your total income (yours or yours plus someone else's if the credit were taken by two people) and they will normally calculate 40% (it can vary from country to country). The credit installments you pay monthly should not exceed that figure of 40%. If, for example, you and your partner earn a total of 5,000 a month, you have a maximum room for debt of 2,000. If you're already paying 500 for a financed car and credit cards for 200, that means that at most they will loan you an amount that yields a fee of 1,300 per month. The bank will also look at your age to calculate for how many years it will be lending to you. There are countries where banks seek that you pay the last installment at age 75, like in Spain. Others look for a different age, based on life expectancy and average retirement age.

Think about all this when you give the bank your documentation and make sure that you are presenting something that makes you more attractive to them. If you can't do it, you may have to find a co-signer that will attract them or generate more income through a low-cost venture and come back again later. They usually review the movements of the last year, so if you're not prepared, in 12 months you can do it again. In any case, ultimately, since we're talking about a loan that you already have and not an application for a new credit loan, regardless of the documents you get, submit the application because there is nothing to lose.

After putting together your document folder as good as possible, present it to the bank and wait for a response. Make a table in which you can see the terms and conditions that they are giving you, and compare it with your current conditions. Let's look at an example of a 200,000 mortgage loan and say it looks like this:

Bank	Interest	Delivery terms	Monthly payment
Current	5%	20	1.314,43
x	3%	30	841,11
y	2,50%	10	1.881,48
z	4%	30	951,66

You must take into account several things in your comparison, especially the interest and the monthly payment. Of course, a lower interest is better, but the delivery term is important because for example in this case, the lowest interest (from bank Y) means the highest monthly payment because of the short term they grant you. You should also ask for information on the additional costs that obtaining that loan may represent, since banks usually give discounts on interest if you take out property insurance, life insurance and credit cards, among others.

Make sure you know the costs that you would have if you terminate your credit with the current bank before the deadline. In the past it was common to find clauses that penalized those advance payments. Also take into account the costs you will have to incur for changing banks, such as notary and taxes, as documented legal acts.

With all this information, the last step is to go to your current bank and tell them that you are considering going to another bank, canceling the accounts and products with them because they are offering you better conditions and refinancing in another bank. Ask them what they can offer you so that you can stay with them. They will almost always tell you that they will think about it and you may also have to provide documentation to do a study; but since you already have it in your folder, everything's ok, the process will be very fast.

Now you have four proposals and on paper you will see improvements in your monthly cashflow. With that monthly cashflow you can start your path to freedom; first freeing yourself from bad debts with high interest rates, then creating a safety cushion, then canceling all bad debts and at the same time, creating savings that will become an investment. Although there are many ways to improve your cashflow starting today, restructuring your debt may be the most powerful, since not only do significant cashflow figures tend to be released, but it also doesn't even involve tightening your belt, or modifying your current lifestyle. It's financial intelligence in action and at full power.

If your current bank is not able to offer you good conditions, don't worry about calling them and giving them a "farewell and talk to the hand". Your new identity no longer goes with that bank, which only wants to impose conditions on you and take advantage of you. Of course, when making the change make sure you read and fully understand the costs related to the change and the fine print, both from your current bank and your future bank. Don't let them fool you and if the decision overwhelms you, you can always ask for the opinion of a professional. This last option can save you a lot of money and headaches. The more time we spend in the business world, the more we realize how important it is to have a good team with which you can consult different topics. Before, we saw it as an unnecessary cost, now we see it as an important savings for the future and an investment in tranquility, because it will save you a lot of headaches and you won't be facing the challenges of business alone.

What is described in this chapter can be applied to any type of credit, and if you have several, you will see how you can free up a lot of money per month in the process. Welcome cashflow! The most important thing will be your ATTITUDE. Remember, you'll never endure financial bullying again. You have a plan and you're looking for those to help you carry it out; you don't want the rest as business partners. #STOP_financial_bullying

MONETIZE WHAT YOU CONSUME

S everal years ago, I came across a concept that deeply impacted me. At that time, they called it "Household Gold"; there's a book by Dr Steve W. Price and videos on the internet with the same name. It was accompanied by the caption: *"How do you turn household expenses into household income and become the owner of your own life in the process?"* What it proposes is very simple but revolutionary and requires common sense to see the enormous potential it has. It's about taking advantage of the new distribution systems that discard the old-fashioned ones of the industrial age. The funny thing is that, at that time, in 2003, when they wrote it, they didn't have the technology or platforms that exist today, but still managed to make use of it in a powerful way. Much less, not even the models of the so-called *"sharing economy"* existed, of which we will speak later. We understood the concept from the beginning and we can say today that it has been a source of thousands and tens of thousands of dollars over the years; not only without downgrading our life but with an increase in its quality, enjoying better products and services from a more fun and practical way.

Let's talk about the concept of household gold, but furthermore, let's talk about how it applies today with new technologies, because with them it's not only convenient to buy but also more comfortable and fun. Today, with everything we have available in the palm of our hand thanks to our cell phones, we can talk about something even more powerful, which is the *"Monetization of your consumption"*. The word monetize is trending. Monetize your videos, your social media, your ideas, and your talent. Here we will monetize your consumption. The idea is this: every day you and your family members use lots of different types of products, and the profit from those products goes to a few members of a traditional distribution chain. With modern distribution systems, such as shopping through apps, we could participate in that economic cycle instead of just contributing. This way, we'll keep part of the profit that otherwise cashflows to third parties and that, over time, can mean the accumulation of huge amounts of money.

Imagine that in the typical old-fashioned distribution chain of the industrial age, in which you go to a supermarket, the products you buy come from somewhere in the world, for example from China, and to get to your house they travel across the whole world. Many hands are involved in this process by global, continental, country, regional, local, city, and neighborhood representatives. All of these individuals have huge expenses and earn money. There are huge storage, transportation, payroll, taxes, insurance, and operating costs. Who do you think ends up paying for all that? That's right ... you and me as consumers. If we also add the investment made by brands and supermarkets in traditional marketing and advertising, the figure rises in an exorbitant way. On average, in the distribution chain, marketing and advertising, take between 70 and 80% of the money. Of course, today there's Amazon and other distribution systems that eliminate intermediaries, so we can buy for cheaper. But in mass consumer products which we're talking about, the price doesn't vary too much and the customer still doesn't receive anything in exchange for their fidelity.

The concept of the gold mine at home is an excellent example, when compared to the real estate market. When you live renting, you can be paying the rental fee year after year, and after 30 years you end up with nothing. On the other hand, when you buy your house with a mortgage, there is a portion of what you pay monthly that goes to the equity of the property, meaning that it's ultimately paid to yourself. After 30 years, you'll have your home. That is … if you have to live somewhere anyway and pay for it, why not do it in a way that gives you something if you have the chance to?

This concept is valid especially in countries where the interests of the purchase of a house are low, and they apply to common properties, not luxury. What we have found is that in luxury properties the rent you pay is very little in relation to the value of the property, and in those cases it is better to not buy. For example, in Spain, in many cases a property of 1 million Euros can be rented for 2,500 per month. Without knowing much about investment, you could get 6% of that million, which is 5,000 a month, leaving you enough to pay the rent and another equally large sum to spend on whatever you want. Also, you don´t have to pay taxes or mayor expenses when you rent.

However, in low and mid-range properties, if you get low interest rates, around 5% or less, what the home gold mine proposes is valid and it's better for you to buy your house than to live renting. It's also valid if you are one of those people who cannot be trusted with money because you make it disappear as if by magic. In this way, paying your mortgage is a way to "force" yourself to save and at least you'll have your house. This is advice for people with low financial intelligence, which are the majority. We hope that through our work of upgrading financial education, many more will awaken and increase their financial intelligence, therefore being able to make better decisions.

In "household gold", they make a parallel with the household expenses. Of each product that you buy for your home, there is a significant portion which is the profit of that chain of intermediation and advertising that we already talked about. What happens if you learn to buy directly from the manufacturer in an intelligent way, through apps and technology? Then, that money which is the profit, month by month stays in your pocket and thus improving your cashflow. That's the purpose of this book. Since you are going to consume your whole life you can accumulate a fortune just with this concept: simply by *monetizing your consumption* and using compound interest. We will analyze it thoroughly in this chapter.

There are companies that for many years have been engaged in this type of disruptive marketing called *"network marketing"* and that prioritize the customer by incentivizing them with money and real benefits, such as savings due to more efficient products and of higher quality, apart from tons of other discounts and monthly benefits for expanding the amount of buyers through generating consumer and marketing networks. It's a win-win business, because by being able to go without that 70% of the money that was previously used in intermediation and advertising, and taking advantage of voice-to-voice advertising which today is exponentially potentiated with social media, these companies also have much more money to invest in scientific advances, research and development.

Their products are usually developed with state-of-the-art technology, respectful of the environment and ethical, avoiding for example, testing on animals, making good use of soils and offering decent working conditions for their employees. By freeing up the enormous costs that the traditional distribution and advertising model implied for these companies, they rescue budgets that can be invested in science and good practices.

You may have heard about these types of companies and may have received negative comments. We must say it's true that there are many companies that claim to be from the Network Marketing industry and are disguised pyramids and fraudulent ponzi schemes, often with dubious products. The success of this industry has caused unscrupulous people to take advantage of its reputation and promote their fraudulent schemes. These types of scams happen in all industries; sometimes, in the stock market and in financial products, they offer false "investments", disguising them as sophisticated financial products, when in reality they are pyramids and robberies. This has happened over and over again in history and an industry shouldn't be ruled out just because of that. Rather, we should learn from it so to separate what is real from what is not and develop the criteria for evaluating business and investment opportunities. With research and information, you can make a good decision and choose a good company with whom you won't have unpleasant surprises later on.

You must check the solidity of the company before associating with any and especially the products should make sense to you. Data such as how long it's been in the market, the high quality of its products and the fact that they have a satisfaction guarantee, are important. Most businesses that don't last long are financial fraud or are based on shady products that no one would normally buy. In other words, the company you choose is based on the consumption of products that you would buy "anyways" somewhere.

These solid companies are part of government associations in different countries. They're usually distinguished by their social contribution and participation in the business and community world. Some of these solid pioneers of the industry have

also experienced enormous global growth and offer their partners and customers an immense range of products from different lines, such as personal care, home care, health, nutrition,
fitness, skin care, makeup, food, beverages, water, home technology and services; the list is impressive. Also, a lot of mayor
companies with good reputation have partnered up with this
companies to sell their products through their networks. This
is a good indicator of how well stablished the company is because obviously companies with valued trademarks would not
associate with them otherwise.

We are going to suppose there's a family of four, for which we're
going to make a small list numbering all the basic and common
products that most of us use every day, just to illustrate what
we are talking about:

Personal care

1. Toothpaste
2. Toothbrush
3. Mouthwash
4. Dental floss
5. Hand soap
6. Body soap
7. Shampoo
8. Conditioner
9. Shaving gel (foam)
10. Shaving Blades
11. Aftershave lotion
12. Facial cleanser
13. Facial tonic
14. Facial moisturizer
15. Eye contour cream
16. Sunscreen
17. Hair gel

Kitchen

1. Dish soap
2. Kitchen degreaser
3. Sponges
4. Dishwasher soap
5. Oven cleaner

Cleaning

6. Floor cleaner
7. Bathroom cleaner
8. Glass cleaner
9. Disinfectant
10. Sanitary Cleaner

Laundry

11. Detergent
12. Stain remover (bleach)
13. Fabric softener

Make up

14. Liquid foundation
15. Powders
16. Eye shadows
17. Concealer
18. Mascara
19. Eye liner
20. Brow liner
21. Lip stick

Fitness and nutritional supplements

22. Multivitamins
23. Omega 3
24. Vitamin C
25. Calcium

26. Veggie protein
27. Casein Protein
28. Energy drinks
29. Fitness: pre-workout, CLA 500, Rhodiola, magnesium
30. Kids multivitamins
31. Kids vitamin C

Also calculate, of how many of these products you have more than one unit in your house, such as toothpaste and soap; you have as many units as the number of bathrooms in your house. The idea is to raise awareness of the immense amount that in a lifetime we dedicate to these types of products. If you only spend $100 a month on these products, they add up to $1,200 a year. If you live 80 years, that's $96,000. Imagine if from that amount, you saved 50% between the savings that these products give you just by being concentrated, more efficient and of higher quality and thanks to your members' discounts. Remember compound interest? With those $50 in savings per month, which will remain or return to your pocket, you already have half a million dollars for your freedom fund!

Look at the first table in the compound interest chapter and ask yourself what was the sacrifice you made? None!.. You are simply being smarter when it comes to shopping. You are *monetizing your consumption*. Now do the exercise with more money, assuming that there are more people at home or that you're consuming other additional product lines. How much can you increase the savings? 100 a month? 200? Go back to the compound interest chapter for a moment and see the wonders you can do with that cashflow "anyways." They are the fortune seeds of your personal fortune.

Something that caught my attention, when I traveled to the United States as a child to play tennis, is that many times for whatever reason may be, I would find a very long line, for example for a buffet restaurant, and next to it there was another corridor where no one was making a line. As I was a child and very innocent, I'd go to where there wasn't a line and would find, fortunately, many times they were also opened and offering the same. Over time, I realized that most people follow a system without questioning it, being influenced because others do it even when having a better option in front of their noses.

People are very afraid of the "what will they say" and they don't want to make a fool of themselves by going to a line that they think is closed because they assume that "it is not possible". They are accompanied by phrases such as "if it were true, everyone would do it". As we grow older and become adults, the more easily the ghost of "what will they say" invades us. We stop questioning the system in which we live in and submit to "what there is". The worst thing is that we don't even ask. I learned that you always have to ask, and that "NO" is the worst thing that can happen. It's ok! And if it seems to someone that this is a reason to criticize, then that speaks worse of the critic than of the person being criticized, as in most cases.

Always dare to face things with a different way of thinking. Are you scared of something? Fear is the absence of data. Ask the questions you have to ask to overcome the fear. Start small so that if you lose, you don't lose too much. You will always gain experience anyway.

The goal of this book is to empower you to thrive. As we have repeated many times, because repetition is the mother of all skills, the key is that you have a positive cashflow so that you can pay off debts, secure your future and go after your financial freedom. From our experience, we recommend these direct purchase systems from the manufacturer, as they can give you an immediate cashflow by *monetizing your consumption*. Of course, be aware of how much you are saving and separate that money. If you used to spend 150 a month on those products and now you spend 100, don't increase your expenses, take those 50, separate them and allocate them to your freedom plan, because we must admit that many times people improve their cashflow through the ***monetization of their consumption***, but they don't perceive that figure because they increase their expenses in other things, generally unnecessary. Having the discipline of separating the money that you are liberating with the practices you are learning, is also an indicator that you are raising your financial intelligence.

SHARING ECONOMY

It's not about having; it's about the benefit or the experience!

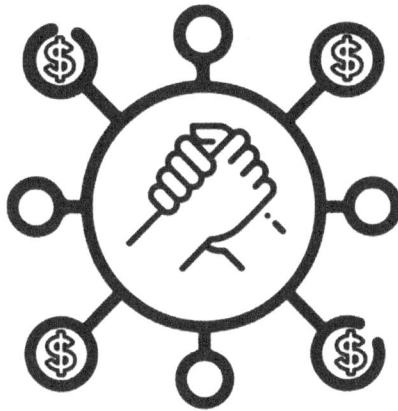

S haring economy applications for cell phones are here to stay. Life will never be the same again. Today we have apps for everything. New generations have discovered wthat it isn't necessary to "have" and that in fact in many cases, it's a headache. Why have a skateboard, a bike, a motorcycle or a car, if there are applications with which you can have access to them for whatever you need, without paying maintenance, taxes and parking costs. The money you can save is significant.

Let's go to a very basic example: when you buy a drill, what you want is not the drill but the hole that the drill makes in the wall. Ask yourself very sincerely how often do you use a drill? What if instead we had access to an app that located us with GPS, to neighbors who own a drill and are willing to lend it for a symbolic donation of $1 a day, wouldn't you prefer that option instead of buying it? That day you'd be able to make all the holes that you needed and save yourself the purchase of a drill. This way you'd also be saving the planet from the manufacturing of another thing and avoiding the environmental consequences that it brings. You can apply this formula or a similar one to other things: bicycles, music, electric scooters, motorcycles and the list goes up every day!

Why buy a vacation home if there are applications with which you can enjoy the experience of being wherever you want and for as long as you want? Did you know that you can even rent a medieval castle in the vineyards of Tuscany? You can go with 12 friends and it costs less than €50 a night, depending on when you go. Now ... can you imagine owning that castle? How much would you have to pay in maintenance, taxes, and employees? Crazy ... I bet the owners rarely use it.

A relative and boat owner told us that for most occasional boat users, there are only two happy days for someone who buys a boat. The day they buy it and the day they sell it, the rest is hell! The maintenance costs and the headaches caused by the constant repairs, make it not only very expensive but also very wasteful, making the time you enjoy it very little compared to the time you spend worrying and fixing it. This is called cost/benefit. Would you like to have all the benefit without the cost? Well, if you like sailing, unless you do it all the time, how about renting the boat when you want to go?

I remember once we bought a jet ski. We had it in a house that had a community lake, 3 hours from the city. We were lucky enough to go once a month for the weekend. We would spend all of Saturday morning trying to get it to turn on, because due to the little use we gave it, it always had ignition problems. In the best case, after a couple of hours, we could get it to turn on or on the contrary, had to take it in for repairs. Many times, we couldn't use it all weekend. We saw that in the community lake club, there were jet skis for rent. One day we got tired of owning that beautiful and unfortunate luxury toy, and not because we stopped liking the experience of jumping through the water at full speed or water skiing, but because we could continue doing so without owning the vehicle. In this particular example, we want to show that the cost/benefit wasn't positive. We could still have the benefit without the cost, which is more attractive.

A very successful and very wealthy dear friend of mine once heard us talking about this topic and felt identified. She told us how she had a beach house in Spain, while living in Mexico. She would go to the house once or twice a year for a month, and each time she would spend about 10 days fixing up the place. Being located on the waterfront, she would find rust in many places, damaged air conditioners, appliances in need of maintenance, windows and doors that no longer opened correctly, blocked shutters, and not to mention the outside. She would end up too exhausted after fixing everything, that all she just wanted to do was rest; but now she only had half the time that she had allotted into enjoying her home. One day she decided to sell it and instead rent luxury properties through different portals. She now enjoys from day one that month of relaxation in the Mediterranean, and what she saves in maintenance, taxes and services is more than what it costs her per year. This was, without accounting for the mortgage payment that in her case didn't exist and the money recovered from the property, released to invest somewhere else.

Today you can experience the best of this world without having to buy it, and that has a very interesting benefit in regards to this books goal, as it is an impressive cashflow release. Think about how many things you have that you don't need and that you could substitute with a sharing economy app. Sell those unnecessary things and calculate how much you will save on insurance, taxes and maintenance. Now add that figure to the calculation of your monthly **CASHFLOW**. Every time, more and more is piling up and you're creating a tsunami of freedom!

FREEDOM CASHFLOW: DETOX FROM BAD DEBTS

I f this is the first time you've seen the term "bad debts," it sure caught your eye. Most believe that all debts are bad, because of the kind of feelings they cause in others. Let me tell you that debt can be good or bad and it is very easy to classify it. Ask yourself, who is paying the debt? If it's you, then it's bad, but if it's someone else, then it's good. For example, if it's a car for your personal use or your home, it is bad debt, because you pay for it. If, on the contrary, it's an investment property for which a tenant pays you rent and that money covers the debt and leaves you with something at the end, then it's a good debt, because someone else is paying for it. In the same way, if it's a car that you rent out to others in any type of way, or for example you benefit from renting your goods on applications of sharing economy, and what you collect is greater than what you pay in debts, it is undoubtedly a good debt. So don't be afraid of good debt, but start with small and controlled debts in which you are sure will pay themselves.

Bad debt is a cancer that begins to appear in people's lives at different times. Getting rid of them is one of the most important *financial detoxes* we can do. Whether it's due to a housing issue, such as a mortgage, a car, appliances, technology or an unforgettable vacation (unforgettable because the credit card reminds you of it every month), debts and interests begin to accumulate in a disorderly way. This generates huge fees and often also unknown costs, such as insurance associated with debt, handling or credit card fees, opening commissions, modification of fees and others that banks keep hidden.

This is something that happens to all of us. In our case, years ago we began to accumulate debt from cars, credit cards, consumer loans and others. We had no idea what interest we were paying on each one, we weren't very sure about the terms and how the amortizations worked either. How much of what we were paying was going into covering interest and how much to capital or principal? We didn't know. The truth is that most of us prefer not to uncover the pot of debt and see what's cooking inside, because we know we won't like what we find. So we take the wrong path, which is to avoid thinking about it because it damages our emotional state, and we let time pass by hoping that, in an illusory way, the situation will resolve itself, which only makes it worse. In life, you have to be positive but that doesn't mean avoiding reality. As Tony Robbins would say, being positive isn't about going to your garden and chanting, "There's no weeds, there's no weeds, there's no weeds", it's about going to your garden grabbing the weed and ripping it out. That's how life is improved and that's what we'll do with bad debts, eliminate them because they are weeds that can damage everything else in our life!

In the reorganization of those debts, there is an immense potential to free up cashflow and to be able to start saving and investing. In this chapter, you will learn how to re-prioritize bad debts and start paying them off with a system. The cashflow that you will release after paying the first one, will accelerate the speed with which you pay the second one and will become a **"FREEDOM CASHFLOW"**, which, like the great liberators of America, began by liberating one country but ended up liberating many others; since with each liberated country their armies grew and thus impacted other parts of the continent, having created a momentum of freedom. In the same way, your **FREEDOM CASHFLOW** will intensify and gain momentum. Then, with the release of the first and second debt, you will go after the third, and so on, until you're done. Then you'll be able to redirect that **FREEDOM CASHFLOW** that was leaving you through debt escapes before, towards your goals and towards your harmonious and bright future.

Are you are ready? We are going to attack them right now. The first thing you should do is organize your debts in a list (you must include those of your partner). Use an electronic spreadsheet or write down all the debts you have, no matter how much or who you owe. I imagine that, if you are like most people, this list will include mortgage, car debt, consumer debt, credit card debts, etc. Put each of these separately, the Visa, the MasterCard, the one from the store, and the one you forgot you had and is stored in some drawer, debt with your parents, family or friends, should also go on the list. Make sure all 100% of the debts are there and also that you have all the information. Sometimes you'll have to call the bank or whoever loaned you the money and clarify the interest, since we have found that many people don't even know how much they're paying. You should also put a column in your list that includes the associated monthly costs, such as insurance, card maintenance fees, etc.

The second thing you will do is put aside the amount you owe today, the fee you pay monthly and the annual interest that they are charging you. When you finish, it might look something like this and you'll be paying, for example, about 2,600 per month, no wonder you have no money to save!:

To whom	How much	Years left	What interest do I pay	Monthly payment	Other cost	Total Month
Mortgage	200.000	27	4%	1000	50	1050
Aunt Maruja	3000	2	0%	125	0	125
Car	25000	5	7,95%	506	40	546
Visa CC	6000	2	19%	219	10	229
Master CC	3000	2	30% (overdue)	255	15	270
Parents	40000	10	0%	333	0	333
Store (TV)	600	2	20%	30		30
Cell phone	800	2	20%	40		40

Now that you have all of them, the second step is to rearrange them by priority. In this method, the criterion for organizing your debts is the interest you are paying. This way, you will put the credit that has the highest interest first. Why? Because interest is the cost of credit; it's the amount of your money that someone else takes. The higher your interest, the more work you're doing for others. The lower the interest, the more of what you're paying that's going towards yourself, to your capital or principal. At a higher interest, what you pay goes towards feeding the bank owners' account. Imagine working hard every month and paying the bank owners' new pool and their trip on private jet! Do you see why you have to pay those with the highest interest first?

This methodology is the one recommended by Kiyosaki and it's the one that we have applied in our personal experiences to get out of bad debt forever. Some authors recommend paying the smallest debts first so that you feel powerful having already paid one of the debts. It's true that we would perhaps recommend it to a child or a shopaholic, thinking that they may relapse, so that, at least during the time that it's applied, they can pay off some of their debts. However, we are aiming for an improved version of you, that you have the consciousness to evaluate this as a change of life and through a change of values, never again allowing yourself to fall into destructive patterns for your finances and ultimately for your life. We believe that you are capable of managing your emotional intelligence, of seeing the larger picture and apart from the small satisfaction of getting out of that small debt, in the long term, it's more important to develop awareness and a life plan that will be better in stopping your finances from bleeding out.

For our table, the reorganization would leave it like this:

To whom	How much	Years left	What interest do I pay	Monthly payment	Other cost	Total Month
Master CC	3000	2	30% (en mora)	255	15	270
Store (TV)	600	2	20%	30		30
Cell phone	800	2	20%	40		40
Visa CC	6000	3	19%	219	10	229
Car	25000	5	7,95%	506	40	546
Mortgage	200.000	27	4%	1000	50	1050
Aunt Maruja	3000	2	0%	125	0	125
Parents	40000	10	0%	333	0	333

Once you have your table reorganized, then we start the attack plan. It consists first in systematically eliminating the debts in which you pay the highest interest, this way releasing the cashflow that was previously paying that debt, and then you'll be able to attack the second one with more force, the third with even more, until you create a tsunami of cashflow, massively cleaning out your list. In our example, first we must pay the MasterCard which is overdue. It costs us 30% in arrears and 270 per month between the fees and the costs. The strategy is the following: of the debts that are between the second place and the last, you will pay the minimum fee allowed in order to stay up to date. In the first, you're going to pay the maximum possible and you're going to make sure that you're doing it with contributions to the principal. You're not going to pay the minimum on that first debt; you're going to pay the most you can. For example, you have a monthly fee of 255; well you're going to pay 500, 700 or 1000, the most you can pay on that first debt on the list. Where are you going to get the money from? Where are you going to get the cashflow to do this? Well, from everything that you're learning in this book, whether it's the savings you'll have in the *monetization of your consumption*, services, generation of additional income through you *low-cost venture* or debt restructuring. That injection of new cashflow that you didn't count on before, applying everything you're learning, whether it is reducing expenses or increasing income, it will attack the cancer of bad debts before anything else, eradicating it from your life forever and giving you your freedom. That is why it is called **FREEDOM CASHFLOW**, because first it will free you from debts and then it will give you your financial freedom.

Let's suppose that, by applying the multiple strategies in this book, you freed up an additional 500 dollars a month with which your army of **FREEDOM CASHFLOW** will start. That means that, instead of two years, you'll be able to pay off your MasterCard debt in the coming months, since you will no longer contribute the minimum of 255 but 755 per month. Assuming that of the 255 only 100 were being allocated to the capital contribution and 155 to interest, in a matter of 5 months you'll be able to eradicate this debt: 100 + 500 (extra per month) = 600 * 5 months = 3000. You will have liquidated this cancer in a few months instead of carrying it around for two years!

What do we do now? Let's go for the second! In our case, it's that TV you bought in installments at the electronic store. Look at the interesting thing that will happen now, having gotten rid of credit number 1, you will not only have the additional 500 with which you started, you will also have the 255 that you had as a minimum payment of the Master CC. Oh, and it comes with a bonus! You're also going to cancel that card and free yourself from the fixed maintenance charge of 15 dollars per month. Your **FREEDOM CASHFLOW** grew to 770 and you'll be able to inject them to the 30 you were already paying in that credit. That is, you will have 800 to pay this debt, when total debt is only 600. You will not only be able to free yourself in a month from this other credit, but you'll also have money (200) to pay for your cell phone, from debt 3. We now released 30 additional that you paid each month for TV. Your **FREEDOM CASHFLOW** goes at 800 and injecting it to the 40 that you were paying for your phone. Guess what? That's another debt going out the window, in just one more month. You had lowered your cell phone debt to 600 and with this payment, like last month, not only did you finish paying it, but again, you had money left over that you can apply to credit number 4, the Visa Card. Excited already? It's barely been half a year and you have already gotten rid of 3 bad debt tumors. That's called momentum! It's like when Daenerys Targaryen freed towns of slaves in the acclaimed Game of Thrones series, and then all those she freed joined her army, making it more and more powerful and giving her the power to free more and more nations.

You'll be able to do much more with your *Freedom cashflow* which is now at 840 per month; the result of the sum of the cashflow of 500 that you achieved from the cashflow release exercises that you learned in this book, added to the fees that you no longer have to pay and the monthly charges you released by canceling these products. All this, added to the 219 that you were already paying for the Visa, is 1059. Assuming that, of the payment you make of 219 per month of this Visa CC, 100 are destined to the capital, you will be applying 940 directly to the capital, each month. By the end of your first year, this poisonous fourth debt will have reached the end of its days and with it the fixed charges that accompany it.

Now let's analyze your panorama one year after starting our system. *Financial detox* is going great! You've eliminated half of your debts. You're sure sleeping better, right? What's even better, you no longer have any major interests that are eating away your life. In the one that you pay the most, you have 7.95%, which is quite reasonable. On the other hand, you have a *Freedom cashflow* of 1069 per month, which has more than doubled, compared to the 500 with which you started. That's a 100% increase in *freedom cashflow* in just one year!

With your **Freedom cashflow**, added to what you were already paying before for your car per month, you can allocate 1,600 to that debt, of which 1,400 will amortize capital. You can finish paying off your car debt in a matter of a year and five months, instead of five years. The most interesting thing is that you can now dedicate that cashflow or a good part of it, into saving and investing and accelerate your path to financial freedom. You can pay your aunt and get rid of that debt immediately and you can also increase what you pay your parents, it will surely make them happy to see their children prosper.

You can take care of your mortgage debt more calmly. If you applied all your **Freedom cashflow** to it, you would pay it in less than 8 years, but you can make capital contributions and amortize without haste. Depending on the country where you live, it's very likely that you'll find more attractive investments that give you a higher interest than the one you pay on the mortgage, so it may be better for you to maintain that debt and simultaneously build your assets. It's a matter of numbers and emotional intelligence, as we saw when we analyzed whether it was better to pay debts, or save and invest.

We still need to talk about something important. If you follow the advice in this book, you can continue to increase your income as you develop a **low-cost ventures** and investments. This will make you have more **Freedom cashflow,** that way paying off your debts faster. There are also ventures and investments in which you will have bonuses, capitalizations and rewards. Depending on your level of debt and personal situation, you can allocate part or all of that money to paying off debt capital. All this will cause your plan to get rid of bad debt in 2, 5 or 10 years, decreasing in half the time!

As you can see, it's possible to pay debts; it's just a matter of developing a system. Now the most important thing: **DON'T FALL FOR THEM** again, you cannot allow that after this excellent work and effort. You can't allow that after having killed your bad debts, they revive like zombies and chase after you. However, if you don't change your values or your thinking pattern, it's very possible that you'll relapse, and in a short time be in financial trouble again. That's why it's so important to not only change what we do, but the way we think and who we are. If you pay off your debts, but continue to be and identify as someone disorderly and poor, you will end up falling into financial problems again; because the waters always return to their level and the level is what you believe about yourself, your self-image. For us, it was very important understanding that, more than an effective method to paying off debts, we first needed a change in mentality. Valuing freedom more than status was crucial. Do you know what they say about the definition of status? Status is buying things you don't need, with money you don't have, to impress people who don't even care about you.

It was vital for us to start leaving senseless consumerism behind and dominating those cravings and need of owning things; understanding the value of money in time and how what you keep and invest today towards your financial freedom will be rewarded with profits, or better said ... with compound interest. What do you prefer, paying for a house and a mediocre car all your life or having a plan with which, in a few years you won't even have to work for anyone again, if you don't want to; but in addition to that you have access to all the luxuries and wonderful things that this world has to offer?

We sincerely hope that the method proposed here will free your finances, but, above all, improve your quality of life and your peace of mind. Definitely a life in which you don't have to be stressed out about money or worry about how you're going to pay a lot of commitments; it's a life in which you can redirect all the energy you once dedicated to that, to much more interesting things, such as your venture or the love for your family. Remember that we are Energy and that we have a quantity of it. Wherever you focus your mind, the energy will flow. Everything you focus on tends to increase in your life.

Imagine if your brain had tubes that connected to the different things or situations to which you dedicate your thoughts. Think as if those situations or ideas were bubbles floating around your mind, and that through focusing, you were able to choose which ones you would connect to your mental tubes. Now imagine that, through these tubes, water flows at a rate that begins to flood those bubbles/situations, making them grow more and more. It doesn't matter if they are "good" or "bad", the only important thing is that you have the ability to increase, decrease or make them disappear. Through your thoughts you direct these "mental tubes" and depending on the emotions you put in them, strong or light, you increase the power of the cashflow going towards them.

We give many names to our emotions; there are the positive and negative. Stress, anxiety, and panic are all synonyms, to varying degrees, to the word fear. Hope, illusion, happiness, faith and positivism, ultimately, are synonymous with Love; Love for that future you want to create. To make it easier to understand and not deviate from the purpose of this book, let's talk only about positive or negative emotions. If the emotion is strong and constant, it increases the power with which we flood the thought bubbles that we have, and make them grow more and more.

We therefore recommend that you take this chapter and apply it with happiness and positive energy. It won't work if you do it with a feeling of burden and helplessness, like "I have to pay off debts." Rather, do it understanding that it's a step in your freedom strategy. Keep your mind on the bright future that awaits you.

I repeat, because you already know that ... repetition is the mother of all skills: the situation, desired or not, in which you spend most of your mental time and to which you dedicate your emotions, will increase without hesitation. If it's in prosperity and in the future that you want, you will prosper. If your focus and mind concentrate on your financial problems and debt, you will not only consume your life energy, but those problems will also grow. Make a conscious decision now that you are going to live a life without limitations, and begin by eradicating the weeds of bad debt. Make a commitment to eradicate bad financial practices from your life. Don't commit to starting this process, commit to finishing it. When successful people make a decision, they are committed to seeing it through to the end. People who never achieve anything important believe that commitment is within starting something. So they promise to pay a monthly gym fee and never go. They commit to starting a diet and it ends when they feel hungry. That is why they leave as soon as the challenges arise, which are fundamental and unavoidable in any growth process. The problem is that they made a commitment to "do something" and not to "be someone else." Don't commit to the process, commit to the result. Better yet, fall madly in love with the result and the process will be fun. Declare yourself a total and absolute lover of the life that awaits you and believe me that, not only will you enjoy the road, but the obstacles you encounter won't even be relevant.

Finally, think about what that person who's living that life you want is like. How's their life? How's their thinking process? What positive habits do they have? What negative habits have they broken off? How is it expressed? How do they treat others and themselves? Ultimately, this is the most important thing, because what we are looking for is to become someone better and grow as a person. There is the real reward, in that improved version; bad debts don't fit in right? Well today we begin to eliminate them. And since you have raised your consciousness and your financial intelligence, you will never fall for them again!

PART THREE

UNLIMITED PROSPERITY

IT'S TIME TO... INCREASE YOUR INCOME!

S o far we've talked about how to lower expenses. Now it's time to talk about the other part of the formula, which is the most exciting: Increasing your income! There will come a point where we cannot or won't want to lower expenses much more and the only way out for a better life is by earning more money. It may even be that you're a young person, who lives with their parents and cannot do much with all the restructuring of expenses that we have talked about so far, because you don't pay mortgages, you don't buy the groceries, you don't have insurance and you don't pay for anything apart from your cell phone. For you, the advantage is that after reading this book, you'll have all the tools to do things the right way from the beginning and always be a guardian of your cashflow. In any case, whoever you are, even if you apply the advice in this book wisely and manage to free up an interesting cashflow or don't have major expenses to cut, we still recommend increasing your income and, above all, developing new sources of income.

There are many ways to do it, but we want to be clear with you about the proposal we make in this book. It's not just about making more money, it is about increasing your quality of life and for that, the relevant thing is not how much you earn, but how you earn it.

In a global crisis like the one generated by the **COVID-19** pandemic, it's clear to many that having a single source of income is an impressive risk. Pandemic aside, we still live in volatile and turbulent economic times. The global crisis was already coming and was predicted years ago, but what happened this year 2020 has accelerated it to unimaginable levels. We tell people that having a single income is like wanting to stand on one leg during a hurricane; it's better to be at least supported on 2 legs, as you'll have much more stability. Faced with a situation like that of 2020, the example is the same, only it's a hurricane with simultaneous tornadoes occurring in synchrony around the entire world and with winds of 300 km/hour. It takes a solid personal financial structure to survive something like this, without affecting the quality of life. Extreme situations help us to show the weaknesses in our way of life, and this pandemic, with all the pain, deaths and tragedy, should make us aware of our true financial situation and what measures we must take to be prepared for any future situation. We can't know if in our lives we will experience something like this again, but we must be prepared. As wise people say, the first time isn't your fault, but the second time is: "...second time it´s on you".

As we saw in the chapter on cashflow, cashflow, cashflow, one of the most damaging beliefs we've come across over the years is believing that making more money, from a single source of income, will solve financial problems. This is a terrible lie that will make you a slave to money and banks. We have found this to be a deeply ingrained belief in the tens of thousands of people with whom we have shared, and that it has to do with the "rat race" that we were sold as children.

Well-known authors tell us about this "rat race": work, earn, spend and fall into debt, which begins between the ages of 20 and 25 and for most, it never stops, until death. They compare it to lab rats running in their hamster wheel all day, and no matter how fast they run, they never move forward. Does that ring a bell? As soon as we start working, expenses start to increase. We need a better data plan, transportation, maybe a car, parking and valet for that car, both in the workplace and at home, appropriate clothing for work, we increase expenses on outings and work meetings and since we earn money and we work for it, we feel deserving of better things, like a more beautiful watch, a better cell phone or whatever. Our expenses increase, and we also want to become independent from our family and have our own place, so we pay rent or a mortgage, vacations to rest from so much work and in most cases, since we can't buy the car, the property, the luxuries and the entertainment, we get into debt. We then use credit cards and soon we are prey to the rat race.

As life progresses, these expenses increase and yes, we're earning more money, but we still spend more and get into more debt. It's like the combo gets bigger as the years go by. Just like when, in a fast food restaurant, they offer you an extra-large combo, with more fries and a larger drink, but you know what? It's still junk food! The same happens as we earn more money. Everything is enlarged and our quality of life doesn't improve, although we apparently have a better "lifestyle" before others. Lifestyle is what others see, but quality of life relates to how you feel about your life.

We know lots of stories of people who look great, smell good and seem to have it all in their perfect life. Later you find out that they're depressed, have fallen ill from stress, have gotten divorced or their children are on drugs because of family problems. Of course, they show off their new car made that year, vacations in Ibiza and their beach house.

I'll repeat it one more time and clearly: It's not about making more money. That isn't going to improve your life. Let's remember Parkinson's Law that we saw in the initial chapters, which says that, when your income increases, in the next 2 to 3 months your expenses increase in the same or greater proportion. As your income increases, the banks see that you're getting paid more and they start calling you offering more cards and more credits, increasing the combo size of the rat race.

As we have reiterated over and over, you already know that repetition is the mother of... all skills, so burn this into your brain dear reader: *it's not about how much you earn, it's about how you earn it.* Earning more money will not improve your quality of life, but earning in a different way will. Kiyosaki made it very clear in his second book "The Cashflow Quadrant." There are four ways to earn, as (E) employee, (S) self-employed, (B) business owner or (I) investor. The problem as an (E) employee or being (S) self-employed is that you're always trading in your time for money. If you're an employee or self-employed, increasing your income means 99% of the time you're working more and having less freedom. In contrast, (B) business owners and (I) investors don't work for money, and their income doesn't depend on the time they dedicate to it. Instead, they have built or bought assets that bring them money every month. If you are a business owner or investor, earning more almost always means having more freedom.

One day, I was talking to a friend from school, after a reunion on social media, 20 years after our graduation. This was the guy I sat with on the school bus every morning. We hadn't spoken in a long time, and I was very interested to know how he was doing, remembering that he was very intelligent. Over coffee, he told me everything he had studied. It was impressive. He had 4 university degrees in different programs such as medicine, economics and anthropology, which he had studied in Colombia, the United Kingdom and USA. I had never heard before the degree of specialization to which he had reached. He had been studying since we had last seen each other, and he continued to do so even to that day. I told him how impressed I was. So I asked him a simple question ... "and how are you doing in life?" Immediately his face changed color, going from pride in all that he had achieved in his academic life, to an expression of overwhelm and hopelessness. He told me that he earned very little, and between what he and his wife made, they couldn't meet their monthly commitments, because their daughter's expenses were high and they paid him very little in his academic work; that made him feel like a bad father and husband.

He knew from our social media profiles that we had a life in which we frequently traveled the world, dined in luxurious places and attended the best sporting and cultural events. He mentioned that he found our lifestyle admirable. Based on this and having told him that I considered him a person of outstanding intelligence and someone with exceptional abilities, I asked him for permission to tell him what I thought of his situation. He accepted.

I told him that in life, we tend to specialize and focus on those things that we do well, because we have a natural talent for them. The one who's numerical looks for tasks that have to do with numbers and analysis. The one who's good with people looks for tasks in which he can interacts with others. That's all very good and it helps develop the potential that each one carries within. The problem is that the art of living is multidisciplinary and human beings are not just a single thing, nor can we define ourselves by a single activity. This is an evil legacy of the industrial age in which we identified ourselves with a profession or trade. It is common to receive only one answer to the question "who are you?" For example "I'm a doctor", "I'm a teacher", "I'm a carpenter." As if we were nothing more than what we do to make money.

I went on telling him that I thought that our lives were like a company with several departments. Just as in a company there's a production department, another for marketing, finance, accounting, sales, human resources, public relations and others. In the same way, in our lives there are several departments, such as the health department, love, relationships, professional development, spiritual, money (note that the "profession" area is different from the "money" area). If in a company one of the departments doesn't work well, or worse, is closed, sooner or later it will end up affecting all the other departments, even those that work in an outstanding way. For example, if the finance department doesn't work well, there'll be no money to finance the other departments or to pay the salaries of those who belong to those departments. Sooner or later, the company's marketing plans for example, will be discontinued, production will stop, the human resources department will receive law suits from employees, the accountant will receive penalties for non-payment of taxes, and the entire company will end up at risk. The same thing happens with our lives. If we neglect health, for example because we are focused on making money or on our professional development or performance as husband/wife, mother/father, sooner or later that neglect of health will cause illness, charging us interest for neglect and it will end up affecting all those other areas of our life where we were putting in effort and dedication. An example that illustrates this clearly is that the most frequent reason for divorce is financial problems, above lack of affection or infidelity. We could use the same example with the spiritual or human relations area, the same thing always happens. Human beings have different needs and meeting only one of them, forgetting the others, will bring consequences.

I commented to my friend that I felt like he had dedicated himself to his profession and academia so such to an extent that he had neglected the money department for a long time in his life, and that now this neglect was taking its toll and affecting other areas of his life, such as his family. I also told him that we were sold lies as children and adolescents; making us believe that the area of money was related to the area of profession and that success in one of those areas is proportional to the success of the other. This is false. We finished our coffee and with pleasure, I saw in the following months on his social media that he was making efforts in venturing. I sincerely hope that he's doing well.

Let's review this one more time because it's very important: the belief that "if I'm a good professional I'll have money" is false, and the examples of people who have succeeded in professional development to fail monumentally in their finances, abound in this world. One thing is one thing and another is another thing. Attention: **THEY DON'T GO HAND IN HAND**. You must attend each one as what they are, separate departments of the company that is life.

If you're like how my friend was, and you're realizing that perhaps there are departments in your life that you have neglected, what is the solution? Well, it's not to start crying for what you haven't done in the past, the solution is to take action and start taking the steps towards the destination you want in any area of your life. The easiest way of doing it is asking, "How is the life I want to build for myself?" "If I could go to the future and see myself fulfilled and satisfied, how do I spend my days?" "What is my family like?" "How much do I earn each month?" "How much of that do I dedicate to savings and investment?" "How is my health?" "How is my spiritual life?" Then we have to ask ourselves much more important questions that we had already asked ourselves in previous chapters, but that are worth reviewing:

What is that person who lives that life like? What skills do they have? How do they think? What habits do they have? How do they treat others? How do they treat themselves? What are their top values?

And the most important in regards to this chapter: How do they earn money? And how do they receive their income?

You may ask, "so… what do I have to do?" Well here it goes: Be that type of person starting today … Easy? Not at all, but… in life you shouldn't do what's easy, but instead what's worth doing. Doing something easy has never brought you any real benefits. Everything that has cost you effort has led you to learn and to be who you are today. This, believe me, is worth it!

Let's go back to the main topic of this chapter and the most important lesson: *it's not how much you earn, it's about how you earn it*. In our seminars, we ask the audience how much they think a monthly figure should look like to allow them to live the life they want. Usually it comes out around $10,000. So I ask them if they know of people who earn that figure as an employee or being self-employed, to which they answer "yes," So I ask them, what do you think the life of an employee or self-employed person is like who earns $10,000 a month? They usually answer that it's a stressful life, with high probability of having health issues and that it's common to find that people who earn that kind of money as employees or self-employed, to have family problems or to be divorced. Finally, I ask them if they had to choose an emoji to describe that life, which one would they choose, and many agree on the one that shows a lot of stress, the one with a drop of sweat or the one with a sad face. Then, I make them reflect on the fact that another way of earning $10,000, is by owning a comercial property in which there is a fast food restaurant that pays $10,000 a month in rent. It's the same number. I continue to reflect on what life is like for that person who owns that place, and everyone agrees that they surely have a high quality of life and that the different departments of their life, such as health and relationships should be fine, since they have time to attend to them. Finally, when asking about the emoji, many choose the one with the happy face or the one with sunglasses. Same number, very different life; do I make myself clear on what I'm trying to tell you?

We almost always end those sections of the workshops with the following question: in addition to the fact that it's evident to expect that the people on the Business Owner and Investor side have more possibilities of a better quality of life, where do you think there are more people who earn those 10,000 a month?; On the Employee and Self-Employed side or on the Business Owner and the Investor side? As to be expected, everyone agrees that as a Business Owner and Investor it's much more common to find people who earn these types of figures and even much more.

In fact ... If you are an Employee or Self-Employed, the laws say that you will pay much more in taxes and you won't have the possibility of taking advantage of tax incentives or bonuses, that you could take advantage of as a Business Owner or Investor. Nor will you be able to deduct most of the expenses that an entrepreneur or investor can deduct. So at the end of the day ... you won't even end up with the same amount of cash by the end of the year.

I can almost hear you thinking... "Yeah, but I'm neither a business owner nor property owner. I don't have money to buy businesses, start them, nor buy real estate." Well, that's what this book is about, dear reader, that you can jump from the E or S side to the B and I side, starting from zero or negative, as most begin, because not only do they have nothing, but they have debts. This book is about creating a new destination where you have businesses that leave profits and investments, either financial that leave dividends, and/or real estate that generate income.

What we're telling you, is that if you're one of those who think negative or in a "realistic" way, we understand you, because we started at exactly the same place. It's normal to find it hard thinking about a future full of businesses, assets and cashflows, since we didn't choose in the past the thoughts, beliefs and ideas that we put into our head. In our subconscious mind, we are the product of a system that wants us to think that success is impossible. We have been trained in an educational program that fosters a negative thinking pattern. In fact, the traditional educational model in most countries, in a very high percentage, still continues to be supported by the foundations of the Prussian educational model, created by and for the industrial era, where the priority was far from being that you build assets or businesses. This educational model only created hard-working and obedient people, capable of enduring an eternal routine, which invited to not question what was established and to prevent creative ideas. It's normal for most to not see it, it's normal for most to not believe it. In fact, even today the current press tends to attack everything that is outside the established model.

If you are lucky enough to be a visionary and want a different life, then prepare to be criticized by others. It's very likely that, unless your family is a family with an entrepreneurial tradition or with assets, they'll tell you that you're wrong, that you're crazy, and they'll even tell you that they are brainwashing you and other types of nonsense. There is a Chinese proverb that says "the nail that sticks out gets hammered down." Why are we human beings like this? Well, I must say that it is normal. On the one hand, those who love you want to protect you and are afraid that you'll mess up. They were educated in the educational model that we already talked about, and the number one motivational value in that model is fear. In school, we were constantly scared of exams, of our teachers, of parent meetings, etc. Everything is part of the preparation, so that we later fear our boss and the institutions; Fear reigns in the adult world. On the other hand, the fact that you want a different life makes them question their own lives and makes them uncomfortable. Remember ... mediocrity is selfish and seeks company. Free yourself from relationships that are not nurturing. Block those "friends" for a while who don't believe in you or your dreams. Like on your phone, mute for a while the groups that don't contribute to your life. You will ask: And the people I love? My family? My mother? If they're not supportive of you, keep on loving them but spend less time with them while building your own success. It's very funny ... they'll later say to you "I knew you were going to do well" and all is forgotten. Don't be surprised that those friends and family, who criticized you, later return and ask you for money and favors. But hey, it doesn't matter; make enough money so you can give them some… It's ok!

Most of the people around you will almost always tell you to focus on solving the immediate rather than "dreaming fantasies." We agree that, if there are economic emergencies, they must be addressed and solved in the shortest amount of time possible, and to achieve this, the shortcut may be to work more hours or get a second job or occupation for a short period of time. But you have to be aware, that this isn't going to improve our lifestyle and mustn't stay there.

The goal of these pages, is to teach you how to increase your cashflow to heal your finances and prosper without impairing your quality of life, and the solution is not to work like an animal and end up affecting your health and your relationships. The real and important solution is that you generate new income as a Business Owner or as an Investor. You're probably thinking that you don't have capital, knowledge or any other resource that your parents or the education of the industrial age made you believe was necessary in order to venture and invest.

We hope that, at this point, even if you don't know how you're going to do it yet, you're still willing to make a quadrant change and go after B and I. We are here to tell you that the world has changed, and that today you can start without have those resources that were necessary in the industrial age. It is known that many of today's largest companies began in garages or university dormitories without any capital. There are concepts such as Crowdfunding that invest in good ideas and startup companies (young companies).

There are ways to start from your home with little or no investment. As an investor, there are also investment options where you don't need capital or a lot of capital. We invite you to get rid of all those outdated ideas about entrepreneurship and investments that you were taught in the past, and allow yourself to plant new ideas about these interesting ways to earn money that will catapult you into a huge cashflow, adventures and wealth. We're going to talk about that next. But remember, it's about creating your own money-making machine, a machine that will accelerate your path to freedom and wealth.

LOW-COST VENTURE – CREATE YOUR OWN MONEY MAKING MACHINE

I n these times that we are living, venturing is a necessity and given the analysis of consciousness that **COVID-19** has subjected us to in 2020, it's clear that venturing is a matter of survival. The millions, who globally have lost their jobs or closed their small businesses or professional practices, make this unquestionable. As we have seen throughout this book, as the restriction increases in the way of earning money in the old economy, doors are opening to generate income in the new economy. The good news is that these doors are much wider than those that existed before, and they allow people who would have never thought of it before, since it was impossible, to build fortunes and above all freedom without any capital or knowledge to begin with.

It's common to hear people say "I don't have money", "there is no money", "there's a crisis". However, if we consider the money supply, that is, the amount of money circulating on the planet, we can affirm with resounding forcefulness that there has never been as much money as there is now. I'll make it clear as a number. There are 60 TRILLION dollars between circulating bills and coins, current and savings accounts on the planet and short term deposits. It's the highest number in the entire history of mankind. The problem, whether you have a tight budget or feel that today's economy is punishing you, isn't if there's money, it's in the fact that you're betting on an outdated way to generate your money. In the income-generating systems of the last century, there's a shortage of employment or most professional jobs of different types. On the contrary, if you bet on new technologies to generate income, there's a lot of money. We will start by exploring the options that have existed for years, to later enter into some of the most current and modern options.

In the book "The Cashflow Quadrant", written before the year 2000, Robert Kiyosaki tells us that on the B side, business owners, there are 3 ways to create a company. The first is to create a traditional corporation-type business. The key, that he refers to as an indicator that a company is a true system, that doesn't depend on its owner, is when it has over 500 employees. In other words, it's a company of a considerable size. If you think about what it means to create a CORP (corporate) type company today, the fact that you have to compete with China, India, and with the industry of your country that has 50, 60, 100 years or more of experience, makes the chances of a successful new business emerging remote. You must bear in mind, that you must first create a system from scratch.

The second option it gives us is to acquire a franchise. Today there is a proliferation of franchises. Given the slim chances of success in the traditional business world and the need to venture, many choose this option. However ... **ATTENTION**... you must be careful! There are many franchises that haven't proven themselves as successful models and that don't have enough time in the market to qualify as good and safe investments.

I remember that a few years ago, when we went to live in Barcelona, every time we'd visit Colombia we would notice the changes that were taking place and that perhaps by being there all the time, we hadn't noticed before. I remember that a few months after establishing our second home in Europe, when we returned to Colombia we saw that close to our house, there was a new gym where they connected you to electrodes, and by means of electricity they stimulated your muscles while you exercised. It promised great results and we decided to give it a try. The surprise was when we returned to Colombia months later, and saw that now there were three different gyms on the same block, with three different brands. They explained to us that they were franchises and that there was a price war between them, so as to capture the market. So the amount we had paid the first time had been reduced to one third. The most shocking thing was that on the next trip to Colombia, all three gyms had disappeared. All in less than a year! Talk about speed in the new economy! It's brutal and ruthless. We understood several things. Although this is just an example, we noticed the same with various franchises of various types, such as food, juice joints, real estate, jewelry, etc. The truth is that franchises are attractive because they are supposed to be "proven" models that offer you a very high probability of success. You're buying a system and that system must be verified, otherwise it is worthless. However, what we have today is an offer of "neighborhood businesses" that haven't been consolidated and opt for the franchise model to take advantage of people's need for entrepreneurship. Meanwhile, franchises that are tested in time, with great chance of success, are extremely expensive and take many, many years to recover the invested capital. They are still a good option, because by demonstrating that they can remain in time, generating profits and adapting to the change in the world, they have value and can provide security. However, even these are not 100% safe and you may find that you invested all your money and time, went into debt in buying them because of their high cost, and even then, you may still fail. It's the corporate world and that's how it works. There are no guarantees of success.

The third option in order to develop a business on the business owner side, that could become a true system, according to Kiyosaki, is Network Marketing. The value that is given to this venture is that it can reach an organization of 500 members or more, like the one talked about in Corporation-type businesses, to consolidate itself as a system, with the advantage that they aren't employees, but a network of independent entrepreneurs, so you can leverage and the overload is low. This system has evolved over the decades, and although it is still very young and innovative, since it isn't even a century old which is very little for any industry, it has demonstrated its strength and effectiveness to adapt to the changing world, and offers a solid and real opportunity for the entrepreneur who is seriously committed to building their own system. Although it's true that the opportunity depends a lot on the strength of the company with whom it is developed, it is shocking to see the evolution of this industry in such a short amount of time. It began by deriving from direct sales as an option in which the most skilled in this area could generate commissions by training others and basing their results on the success of the sales of those pupils, thus generating income according to the depth levels in which they were developing. That's where the term "multilevel" derived from, a term that in our opinion doesn't do justice to what the most advanced companies of today are developing, relying on technology and social commerce, but the term MLM (multilevel marketing) continues to group many companies that are in different stages of evolution.

Today, in addition to the 3 options that Kiyosaki presents in his classic books, there are different ways of venturing and investing at a low-cost. We will discuss a couple of them in the following chapters, but let's start with the modern and current view of his third recommendation, a real low-cost venture.

TODAY'S NETWORK MARKETING: MONETIZE YOUR SOCIAL MEDIA

I n the 80s and 90s there was a change in the top companies of the Network Marketing industry, in which they began to prioritize leadership over sales. They found that there was unlimited potential in building huge organizations around the globe and generating huge income by building their own business. This began to attract prominent professionals and businessmen of all kind, and gave them the ability to create their own assets without leaving their profession. Since then, it became common to hear stories from professionals such as surgeons, lawyers, restaurant owners, engineers of all kinds, owners of hair salons, builders, senior executives, stockbrokers, who said things like "I'm very successful in my profession, but I also decided to start up my own company or my own asset. I did it for the freedom that this type of business can offer me, because, although I earn a lot of money in my profession, I don't have the time I'd like, to enjoy my family and my success." Accompanied by this change, came a transformation also in education, and in the training received by members of the industry, in what today is called "soft skills", such as emotional, commercial, financial and social intelligence, leadership and influence. This change was very attractive to the market, as they were skills that were not being taught anywhere else and were becoming increasingly valuable in the world. That's why Kiyosaki himself has dedicated valuable books to the industry, such as *The Business School* and *The Business of the 21st Century*. The most valuable thing about this educational program was and continues to be that the teachers aren't theoretical but practical and have applied what they teach in their lives, generating positive results. The growth was massive and began a proliferation of companies in the industry, which, like today's franchises, for the most part didn't remain in time, because they didn't offer a real product, didn't have a solid financial foundation or didn't count with the educational platform.

With the entry of the internet, another era began throughout the world and also in the **Network Marketing industry**, making manual and complicated processes such as checking the status of the network and placing group orders, was simplified and done individually. While the Internet transformed many industries, making businesses of different kinds close when they became obsolete, this new revolution boosted Network Marketing businesses. Once again, the industry demonstrated a high capacity to adapt to global changes and took advantage of the change in trends. Then, with the entry of social media, platforms used to hold virtual meetings, and communication tools such as communication apps and groups, the expansion continued throughout the world. In today's business, there has been a boom of young people in the industry who are not only leaders, they've become also influencers who leverage themselves on different social media and have a global impact. Just think of a simple example; In the 80's to inform the team or promote something, you had to pick up the phone and call each individual member of the network, while today with a message in a group chat, from your phone or from a publication on social media, you can reach thousands and hundreds of thousands in less than a second. On the other hand, through a free video uploaded on YouTube, we can train tens of thousands online and create live events simultaneously with different continents, sharing about the opportunity and launching of strategies, products or techniques, without the restrictions that it implies having to do it in a physical and limited space.

That is why today we can, as we did before when talking about the monetization of consumption, talk about a monetization of contacts and social media of an entrepreneur in this industry. This is a term that we can easily understand today, as we have examples everywhere. In a simple way, you can start earning money by adding value to something that you previously developed for free, such as uploading videos to the internet, recommending products or services, or contributing content on specific topics. The Network Marketing industry or social commerce, as some call it today, can be summed up in three words: monetize your networks.

In the past, the way in which businesses developed, many times involved people who in a titanic task had to go 1 by 1, physically contacting and prospecting people to present them the business in a face-to-face way, either in a group or individually. Many times with high levels of intensity that could annoy the prospect or performing tasks of little prestige, such as handing out flyers in public spaces and similar activities. This old model that many knew and for which they dislike the industry, has disappeared in the top companies and has been replaced by technology, modern videos and digital tools that have more to do with attracting those who are looking to venture than chasing after those who aren't interested.

As the world turns digital, many old-guard traditional companies, across all industries, are at risk of disappearing. What we see in the Network Marketing industry, or whatever name it's given today, is that it continues its evolution and that along with change it incorporates new ways of doing business and expands its advantages. Today, in a world where the roads of the main cities are collapsed, pollution reaches levels never before seen, diseases turn into epidemics or pandemics in record time and ordinary people have less and less time, the development of the Network Marketing business in a digital way, without leaving home, becomes part of its value proposition and gives anyone the possibility to venture from home, Monetizing things that they've always had and will continue to have, such as their consumption of essential products, their relationships, their contacts and the time they spend online, expanding their network and promoting their products and services.

On the other hand, in the age of the tribes, as Seth Godin says, people are moved by ideals and want to follow people who embodied their beliefs. Network Marketing adapts to such a point that the entrepreneur can promote what is important for him. Be it a young man who wants to live without schedules or bosses, travel the world with the freedom of digital nomadism, or take their business on their cell phone. Or a mother who wants to spend more time at home with her children, without this meaning being less productive or not generating income. Network Marketing is also good for a retiree or an elderly person, who finds that the job market discriminates against them and isn't interested in hiring them. Here, they find the possibility of venturing and becoming someone who contributes and is worthy in society. Likewise, it's good for an average worker who knows that by continuing doing only their usual job, they'll never go beyond surviving and paying their debts and bills, tied to a system that will continue to stifle them. Instead, it will allow them to develop a parallel income that gives them flexibility and the possibility of breaking free from that job, with a better income from their own business. Network Marketing is also good for the top executive who earns a lot of money, but doesn't have time for their family or who wants to diversify and create other sources of income and especially their own assets that won't depend on a third party.

The resistance of this type of entrepreneurship, in the face of crises, is one of its strengths. Even in the most critical moments of the pandemic, the top companies worldwide not only remained open, but also grew in percentage terms in their sales. Being low-cost, being based on essential products (or "anyway" products, as we saw in the chapter "Monetize your Consumption"), allowing to operate the business from home, having the ability to develop digitally in an easy way and count in many cases, with a portfolio that strengthens the immune system and is environmentally friendly, gathers many of the keys necessary to succeed in these times. Also, by not having fixed expenses that absorb you, you cannot go bankrupt.

We saw many businesses close during the Covid-19 crisis. Their high monthly expenses, such as rent, payroll and services, brought them down as they were unable to operate as they normally would. That doesn't happen with a social commerce business, as there is no liability or expenses of this type. Over the years, this same constant of sustained growth has been seen in times of crisis. The same happened in 2008, the fall of the twin towers in 2001, the real estate crisis of the 1990s, and the Vietnam War. Time and again, the industry has shown that the crisis benefits its growth, making it an excellent option to create a second income that will sustain itself when others falter.

It's in this adaptability that we see immense potential in Network Marketing and we firmly believe that anyone who is willing to work it as their own professional business, with dedication and perseverance, even without leaving their primary source of income, will be able to build their own network; because unlike the other two options, where one creates the system in a company, as in a traditional Corp. business, or buys a system, without knowing if it will be successful, such as a franchise, in Network Marketing you become part of a system that already works and that has already given results to others, equal or greater than the same results that the new one wants to achieve.

The benefits are huge and diverse. They have to do with the leverage that this type of business allows you. You leverage yourself in money, in the knowledge and time of others, as well as in the technology with which you can have a global expansion. To begin with, the whole model is based on leverage. Once the business takes off, you put in a 1% effort of the 100% of the results and it can become 1 per thousand of the effort compared to 100% of the results. Depending on the company, we have found that the best ones offer you to start with very little money; figures with which you could not start any other business, even the simplest ones. The investments are so low, that they wouldn't be enough for you to register with the chamber of commerce of your city or cover the notary expenses involved in opening a company. Why is this so? Because, although there is a large investment, you don't put in any of your own money, instead you leverage with the capital of the company. Also, the monthly expenses are minimal. You couldn't even pay for the utilities of a traditional business with what it costs to run a Network Marketing business. The income potential is unlimited and if the company is solid and is in several countries, it allows you to expand in other markets and produce income in different currencies, giving you multiple sources of income within the same business and diversifying the risk. Can you imagine living anywhere in the world and producing money, not only in the local currency of your country, but also in dollars, Euros, sterling, yen or any other strong currency in the world?

Another huge advantage is that while you earn money, you

build your asset. Unlike producing money for example with a new economy app, where you can be handing out food all your life, driving passengers in a car or renting your sofa couch, but without building your own company. Here you can also earn money, but in the process you build your own asset, and that's what has the most value. It's an asset that in solid companies in the industry, you could inherit or even sell, but above all has an unlimited prospect of growth.

Also, as you grow, you'll become a mentor for others, with the possibility of impacting people's lives and giving global digital or face-to-face conferences; aimed at groups of entrepreneurs who will be excited to hear your experience and be filled with faith thanks to your teachings. Traveling the world, spending quality time with your family, living in luxury properties, driving high-end cars, supporting foundations for children or the elderly in your country, helping your family, being recognized and transcending, are some of the real possibilities achievable with this business model. We find different people who have achieved this and much more, some becoming true icons of the industry and becoming extravagant, traveling in private jets, attending the most important global events with VIP treatment and being part of the local entertainment. Beyond this, which for some may be superfluous, you can be part of an industry in which your success is based on serving and helping others by bringing hope and empowering them to develop their greatest potential. As many say, it is an industry full of "bright eyes", because it reignites the dreams that people have in their hearts. In addition, it is a project in which personal growth doesn't stop and it's normal to find people who have been doing it for decades and continue to be excited about what is coming. This is a substantial difference with respects to what happens with most of the activities in which we see bored people after a few years of developing their work.

From the point of view of a financial coach, that being the purpose of this book, one of the greatest advantages that we find in this type of company is that, within the same venture, you can generate multiple sources of income. The best companies pay bonuses and income for different aspects. This is how you can generate money by marketing products or services, by the network that you are generating, by monthly and annual incentives for growth, more income from the development of leaders and structures within your network and also for mentoring and training other fees, with different periodicity, depending on the company you are part of. Can you imagine? They are 2, 5, 10 or 15 different ways to earn within the same enterprise. This will allow you over time to separate that income and allocate each one to something different. For example, you can live on the income from your network, dedicate the sales income to your education and growth, leave the annual bonuses to invest in properties, use other income for your vacations and luxury purchases or even better, donate part of it to a cause you believe in. That is, by combining the success of your venture with financial intelligence, it's almost inevitable that you'll become rich if you choose to become a professional.

What About Bad Reputation?

It's common to find that the industry or the name of a company itself generates negative comments or is harshly criticized. The truth is that much of this predisposition is associated with old paradigms that don't fit the current reality or a concept such as *monetizing consumption and social media*. Many enthusiastically start their way in Network Marketing to find that their family and friends tell them that they'll be fooled, that it's a pyramid and that they'll lose money, because they or someone else already tried but didn't succeed.

One of the most important *financial detoxes* we can do is to free ourselves from negative paradigms and neuro-associations that lead us to prejudge the opportunities that are presented to us. In life we associate things that happen to us with pain or pleasure; however, most of the time these neuro-associations are false and were determined by emotional circumstances of the moment. It has happened to all of us that we think we hate a certain food and just seeing it or smelling it causes us disgust. However, at some point we try it again and it turns out that we do like it, causing us great surprise. This happens because probably when you were a child, something happened when you ate that food, maybe you were sick or your parents were fighting, or you had problems with other kids at school. What you were left with, was a negative association between that food and your feelings. That is a neuro-association. It didn't have to do with the food but with how you felt. The same thing that happens with food happens with people and with businesses; we can feel aversion without just cause.

On the other hand, paradigms are the way we perceive things, the mental filters that we have, and they don't respond to how things really are. Imagine this great example that I once heard: a person who doesn't behave very well with their peers, has enemies and is used to insults, is driving his sports car at 200 kilometers per hour on a mountain. When passing by another car, someone sticks their head out the window and yells out: "ASS". Our character feels insulted and returns the insult, but after crossing the next curve crashes head-on with a donkey (also called... ass). Whoever yelled "ass" at them, wanted to save their life, but because of his personal history, because of his paradigms, he took it as an insult. The same thing happens to us many times in business. A negative past experience, yours or someone else's, should not determine your future or your decisions. You could miss out on the best things in life because of paradigms.

There are several reasons to explain why this bad reputation exists and if we are going to consider venturing in this industry, we must understand the implications that this has. First of all, we have found that most people judge the business by the person who introduces it to them or by someone they knew at a certain point in their lives, which was involved with such a company and was projecting a negative image of the business. It's very likely that the same thing would have happened to us, the authors, if we had found ourselves in our jobs, which was trading stocks in a major bank and in television production, and someone with a not very entrepreneurial image and low self-esteem had contacted us with the vision of "recruiting" us into their network. Truth is, they would´ve had very little chances of making a successful contact. This is just how the world works.

Our experience was different; the person who contacted us was someone with high credibility, professional, a businessman from the world of finance and a writer. At all times, we thought that if someone like this person was developing this business, it was because it had to be good. However, this doesn't happen to most people and they are approached by an unemployed person, without much success in life and that makes them skew their opinion and not really want to understand their venture. For this reason, it's important that, when analyzing the possibility of venturing in this industry, you not judge the business by the messenger, instead document yourself, read, listen and then meet the team leaders and see if their vision fits yours.

Another important reason why the industry has a controversial image is that anyone can join this type of business; neither a resume nor your criminal record is required. This means that, no matter how good the company is, the people who develop the business can carry out bad practices and give the company and the industry a bad reputation. Thus, over the years, various people have used company networks to promote political and religious ideals, secondary businesses and even bad money practices. These people have been expelled from the companies and have had their contracts canceled due to their lack of ethics and deceptive practices and today are dedicated to criticizing the industry after having abused it. However, the damage they did was considerable. I must say that this happens in any industry and it is no reason to rule it out, far from it. It would be like choosing to never own a car or letting automotive business opportunities pass by, just because famous brands in the automotive industry developed bad practices, tampering with carbon and other gas emission tests. The same happens in the financial market in which many have carried out fraud, and that isn't a reason to avoid the industry.

There is practically no industry in which scandals haven't existed over the years and in which people have committed unethical acts. The problem isn't in business models or industries; the problem is in people, in their lack of principles and values where they put money before the benefit of society and are blinded by greed. If you're going to develop a business of this type, we recommend getting to know the team members and their leaders. You must know how long they've been in the company and review their trajectory and image. I'm not talking about the person who is inviting you, who may be starting out and have the best intention; I'm talking about the leadership structure that supports it. The Top Leaders of the team. It's common to find that the people who lead the fraudulent companies, that pose as Network Marketing companies, have controversial pasts, come from companies that no longer exist and have even had problems with the law.

As the third ingredient of these reasons for controversy, we find frustration as the protagonist, a feeling that is common and transversal in every industry. Thousands of companies are registered in city chambers of commerce every year, only to find that a few survive after 5 years. All the others get left behind and many never even get to open their doors to the market. Network Marketing is no different in this respect from traditional businesses: only a percentage of those who start will be successful. It's common then, to find people who were excited to build fortunes, now expressing their frustration because the business didn't meet their expectations. When analyzing their experience, most of these people blame the company or the people who were part of their network, but they rarely reflect on their own skills to venture and lead teams. Network Marketing isn't magical. Only the best survive and succeed. When I got to know the industry, I remember being introduced to a great entrepreneur in it. The opportunity was given and I asked him how many of those who enter are successful, and he sincerely replied that only a few, a small percentage of a single figure. I was about to leave when he told me I was asking the wrong question. Of course I asked him what he meant and he told me that the correct question was: "how many of those who work professionally in this business, following the recommendations of people who already have results, becoming professional (as in any activity) and working on it as a serious long-term business, were successful?" In that case, the number is very high, compared to any business.

I understood then that business is neither good nor bad; the key component is the entrepreneur who makes the business work. This is true in all industries. Where some fail, others succeed. In industries such as cell phones, there are people who sell minutes on the street and live in poverty, and there are also corporate titans who have created empires and unlimited wealth. The key is the entrepreneur and his vision. The good news is that you can find these great visionaries in companies and what's even better is that you can be one of them. If the company has a powerful educational program that focuses on developing you as a leader, strengthening your influence skills and personal growth, then you can do it.

Finally, in face of the boom in this type of businesses, many companies of dubious reputation have proliferated, that resembling the serious and established companies in the market, claim to be part of an industry or disguise themselves as part of it when they really aren't. This is how, many years ago, we began to notice that companies appeared in the market promising enormous benefits, but disappeared in a short amount of time, taking people's money and being closed down by the governments or flying the country.

ATTENTION! If you're going to dedicate your time to a Network Marketing business, make sure you know very well who'll be your main partner: the company. It's important that you thoroughly review their history, their numbers, their stability throughout the years, their awards, their social contribution, the practices they use in manufacturing, the type of products they make, their ethics and social responsibility. Also check the laws that regulate the industry in your country and understand precisely the points that make a company constitute itself as a real and legal company. You'll find things like that a solid company must have real products, not strange things that are difficult to understand, and that the money comes from a commercial displacement of those products in your network and not from registering people, like the pyramid type. You'll also see that the registration cost must be low and the products must have a satisfaction guarantee. All those things will help you detect if they're offering you something that is legal and reliable. There are companies that, when you review them thoroughly, you'll find that they are exemplary and their real contribution is far from the perception that some have of it.

I hope you understand now why we find negative comments with respects to it. The most important thing is you understand that this will happen to you with any venture and that this shouldn't be a reason to give up. It's normal to feel scared when starting something new. Fear is lack of information. Study the company and the people who are sharing with you this opportunity with a magnifying glass, and if it is your thing, then start with attitude and determination, looking for a long-term result with a broad vision. We always suggest making a commitment of at least one year, which will mostly be learning, to begin to professionalize and understand this industry. Avoid being impatient and anxious as this can work against you and how attractive you are to your prospects.

And hey! if it's not your thing, there are other options for entrepreneurship and low-cost investments that exist today, with which you could create your money-making machine. We'll share with you below some of the ones we have known and developed, although we know that there are many more. Now that you have a business attitude and vision, we don't doubt for a second that you'll find the one that best suits you.

LOW COST REAL ESTATE INVESTMENTS

R eal estate investments are considered one of the best investments that can be made. Its stability, its value over time and the possibility of creating constant income, make many aspire to have real estate and, having them in an investment portfolio, is an indicator of wisdom and prosperity. In addition, they're one of the investments in which you can leverage the most, taking into account that traditional banks are willing to lend you most of the money to buy them, if you grant them the mortgage on the property. If banks do that and aren't willing to do it with other types of investments or assets, at least in the same percentage, it means that real estate is one of the best assets you can have, as banks know a thing or two about money. Normally, a bank won't lend you money to invest in the stock market, unless you guarantee the loan with other types of assets. They also won't lend money to a new business recently registered. On the contrary, they will get sums of 70, 80 or sometimes up to 100% plus expenses, in certain real estate investments, depending on the country you invest in.

Many, however, refrain from learning about real estate investing because they believe that it takes a lot of money to do so, or because they see the price of properties and consider that it is impossible to participate. Having capital is an indisputable advantage, but it's not the only way to invest in properties.

An excellent example, a modality that exists and is gaining strength is **RENT TO RENT**. That is, you rent to rent to others. For example, you get a rental property and sublet it to someone else, like a 4-bedroom property that you rent for $800 and then rent out each room to students, between 300 and 400, giving you a total of 1,400. Each month you will have a juicy profit and the best thing is that it wasn't necessary buying the property or having annual taxes, nor the exorbitant costs for the purchase and closing costs. Of course, you must do it with the owner having knowledge of the matter and commit to take out insurance and whatever is needed with full responsibility. There will be owners who refuse to do so, but there'll be others who will have no problem, especially if you take care of the maintenance, pay what they ask for on time and not give them any problems. The key is for the owners to see that you know what you're doing and that you act professional. Why buy the property if what you want are the benefits? How many properties could you have like this? You can have as many as you can find, because you don't have to put your own money in any, except maybe buying some furniture and decoration.

I was twenty-five years old and Cata twenty-three, when we did our first real estate business. It was a construction project that to us seemed to be located in a very good area and could be of high demand. The sales room had just opened, and prices were starting at about $25,000 per apartment. With the equivalent of $200 we reserved ours, which Cata meticulously chose out, taking into account the height, the view it would have, the lighting and its position with respect to the sun. The project would take 18 months to build and in the next 90 days we had to complete the payment of 10% for a total of 2,500 dollars, that is, 2,300 additional to what we had already put down. 180 days later we had to put another 2,500 and at the end, 270 days after the reservation, another 2,500 additional to complete the 30% and request a credit for 17,500, equivalent to the remaining 70%.

The real estate market at that time was expanding after emerging from a multi-year crisis, and in the following 90 days the price had already increased by $5,000, for a total of $ 30,000, which was the new price of apartments like ours. At that time, and aware that we should put in the additional $2,300 that we were missing, we shared with some friends who were also interested in real estate investments about the incredible valuation we had had in just 90 days and the projection that the valuation would continue, because there was a lot of demand and there were fewer and fewer apartments. We sold them half of our share at a discount, which now had a value on paper of 5,200 (5,000 of the price increase plus 200 we had invested); they were willing to pay the total of 2,500 of the initial 10%, to go as 50-50 partners. They gave us 2,500 dollars, we paid the 2,300 that we had to complete as part of the commitment with the construction company and we recovered our 200.

For them, the analysis was as follows. The property had a value of 30,000 and after the payment they would make of 2,500, they would still owe the construction company 22,500. The equity of the four of us, the buyers, was $7,500 ($30,000 of the new value minus 22,500 owed). Since they owned half the business, they would own $3,750. They had an immediate 50% profit on their investment. Offering them that immediate profit on paper was important for encouraging them to participate.

As for us, the investment had been reduced to 0 and we owned 50% of the valuation of the apartment, that is, $3,750, just like our friends-partners. Best of all, in the next 90 days the apartments were almost entirely sold out. So, we asked the promoter saleswoman to tell us if there was anyone interested in an apartment on the fourth floor, where we had ours. We got a buyer willing to pay 37,000 for the apartment after negotiating (we asked for 40,000 and he offered 35,000). By selling before the deed, there were no notary expenses, and except for a tip that we gave to the sales person who referred us, we had no more costs. The new buyers paid the $2,500 that needed to be paid to the construction company, and they kept the property after giving us a total of $14,500 which was what our principal or equity of the property was worth at the time (37,000 sale minus the 22,500, which we still owed the construction company).

Upon settlement, our friends took out $7,250, got their 2,500 back, and made a profit of 4,750. Their profitability was 190% in 90 days (760% annualized) and they were happy and eager to do more business with us. To this day, we are great friends, with whom we have ventured and invested in various projects.

For our part, taking into account that the only money that came out of our pocket was $200, we received another $7,250 clean, because our investment had been recovered in the first 90 days, when our friends joined as partners. This is a profit of 3,625%! You read that right, almost four thousand percent, in 180 days or a 7,250% annualized profit! In fact, since we had already taken out the 200 dollars in the first 90 days. From that moment on, we enjoyed what is known as an infinite profitability, since our money was no longer in the investment.

From that day, we fell in love with real estate and understood that the key is in the ability to find good opportunities, rather than in the property itself or even in having the capital.

WARNING: what we did in this case only works in markets where the real estate sector is expanding and this can change suddenly. It isn't the way we invest today, but we use it as an example so you can see that it isn't necessary to have a lot of money and that a large part of the result depends on the way you structure the negotiation and financing of the property.

Like this, we have done several businesses over time with some variations. For example, we bought properties that we remodeled and did a facelift to, inserting some design ingredients that made it more attractive and eliminating everything that made it unattractive, then selling it at a 30% higher in just a couple of months. We have also found properties in which we've made a promise to purchase with a deposit, but have stipulated in the contract that, in addition to being subjected to financing, we could change the final buyer to a third party who could be a natural or legal person, giving us a period of 60 or 90 days to find a buyer. We've done business in which, in those 90 days we resold the property or rather our position in the business or the option of buying to a third party, for several thousands more. Since little money is put down comparatively when signing a deposit, the profitability is enormous. For example, buying a property for $80,000 and making a deposit of 8,000, to then sell it to a third party before the deed, for 100,000, with a profit of 150% in less than 60 days (we won 20,000 and invested 8,000).

It's also possible to do real estate deals in which you enter without capital, getting investors to put in the money and you go in participating with a percentage of the operation and even having part of the property. In these cases, you don't put in your money either. For example, you get a property at a market value of 60,000 for 45,000. You get an investor who wants to buy it for 52,500 and you give him 2 options. You can charge a commission (finder's fee) for having found the property, or you can propose that you also be an owner at a lower percentage. I'm not talking about setting up a real estate agency and commissioning real estate properties. Nor do I urge you to become a real estate agent. I'm talking about you being a real estate detective, a specialist in finding good deals and profits.

Later we discovered that this type of operation is called "*flipping*" in real estate language, which consists of finding something that is going to increase in value, either because the real estate sector is expanding, or better still because it is below the price of the market, or because you can add value to the property or to the perception of the business opportunity with marketing and projection. Understand that, many people who want to invest don't know what to do with their money or they don't have the time to search. There's a lot of value in becoming good at finding these types of opportunities, even if you don't have the money.

Trust me; money is going to flow to you because it always flows to good opportunities. There are great real estate opportunities out there, in any market, no matter if it is a bull, stagnant or bear market. Many people don't see a good real estate opportunity because they didn't like the paint on the apartment, the bathroom, or the floors. If you or someone on your team learns to have vision, they'll detect opportunities where others don't see, and with a few simple changes they'll increase the value significantly, by 15% or 20%. Since we're talking about big numbers, we're talking about a lot of money. It may also be that the property isn't getting the best use, for example, as a traditional rental for holidays, for rooms or for students. It requires someone with vision to find the property, structure the business, and then sell it or invite others to invest.

In countries where interest rates are too high, as is often the case in Latin America, the best real estate businesses in which you can leverage are in making this type of flipping investment, taking into account that you only have the property for a short period of time, and therefore don´t have to pay a lot of fees or interest. For example, in Colombia, rent goes from anywhere in between 4% to 6% per year of the property value. However, banks lend you over 10% per year. Depending on your credit score, it can even get closer to 20% per year. That means that for every peso they lend you, you are losing money (they lend you at 10 and you rent at 6, you have -4%), and that is why it's normally not attractive to buy to rent long-term with mortgage credit.

In the United States and Europe, the opposite occurs. Banks lend at very low rates and you rent at a much higher percentage. For example, now we have some loans in which they lend us at 1% per year and we have rented the properties at 7%. It is worth leveraging because for every euro they lend us, we get + 6%.

It is important to understand that conditions vary in each country depending on taxes, mortgage conditions, and market cycles, as well as supply and demand. That's why we'll limit ourselves to giving you some basic principles that work anywhere, and we'll leave it up to you to find out the details of your local market and country if you want to bet on real estate investments. In other spaces such as workshops or future books, we will share more about real estate strategies based on our experience. For now, we share 3 keys.

Key #1. 100:10:3:1

This principle has been shared by the gurus of the real estate market and it means that out of 100 properties that you analyze, you'll put offers in 10, negotiate in 3 to buy 1. We have verified it and it really works like that in practice. You must define the type of property you're looking to invest in according to the use that you're going to give to it. Do 100 sound like a lot to you? Imagine that before, there were no real estate portals on the internet and you had to go looking one by one, taking your own photos to then analyze. Today the truth is that we have it very easy. It just takes a little discipline and that's it. In any case, that property that you keep, you'll have for all your life ideally. It is like a marriage. Therefore, the key for it to be successful is to do the work, researching and reviewing all the information.

Be careful with this: *trust, but verify*. Did they tell you that a property is rented out every month? Check it out. Remember that the seller wins because you buy the property, not because you make money with it or because you have good profits. That's your problem. Are the community expenses up to date? The tax payments? Are there pending payments or extraordinary fees to pay for building works or expenses? Check the invoices. Did they tell you that the neighbors are nice and quiet? Check it out. Ask to see the files of neighborhood meetings and check for complaints. Knock on neighbors doors on different floors, identify yourself and ask for their experiences. You'll be surprised at what people are willing to share. Talk to whoever presides over the neighborhood community and with the administrative office. Collect as much information as possible so that you are not buying a problem.

We were recently on the verge of buying a property in Zaragoza, but upon visiting it and talking to the neighbors, we learned that there were some troublesome neighbors. Reviewing the files of neighbor meetings, we found that a tenant of one of the residences has had mental problems for years and scares the neighbors, there are suspicions of drug trafficking and also those who live there are untidy, because the bad smell reaches the elevator. Those who have entered the residence of the troublesome neighbor say the property is destroyed. This diminishes the value of the entire building of apartments. If we hadn't done our research and had blindly believed in the commercial agent, who I must say was a good professional and had the best intention, we would have bought a very expensive headache.

Key #2. The Money Is Done When You Buy, Find The #Nowanters

We don't believe in the real estate investment deals where you sit and wait (pray) for valuation. Many people believe that being an investor is buying from blueprints in a construction sales office. Many times, in these projects they give you chocolates, coffee and if you buy from them they'll give you the keys in a very nice box, a beautiful folder and a key chain. We have a saying: "if it comes with a doll, someone else takes the toll". Who do you think pays for all that, for the showroom, the salaries, and everything else? You are right; it's you as the buyer. In this type of project, except for some special situation, someone else has already made the money and the buyer is the last to enter the scene, paying for a long chain of beneficiaries. In other words, you're almost always buying above price. You can no longer generate value to a property like this, and, we repeat, the money is in generating value. The business must be good even if the properties don´t go up in price.

There are two types of businesses; the dairy cow businesses (which generate cashflow) and the beef cow businesses (where you expect to sell after the price goes up). The problem with the beef cow businesses is that to make money you have to sell the asset (kill the cow). Although it's good at the beginning to do business like the beef cows, looking to expand your capital, the ideal is to have many dairy cow type properties and live on the income of these properties. Imagine what a delight to have a building with 60 units, each generating between $800-1200 per month. Every month, whether you work or not. That's what's called living on true residual income.

The *flipping* businesses that we have mentioned are beef cow businesses and work very well in expanding economies. They can also work very well if you learn to hunt for opportunities, not only in times of expansion but at any time. That's why it is said that, in real estate investments, money is made by buying. It's referring to the fact that you must find the property that, despite being an excellent asset, is covered with a dark layer that doesn't reveal its potential. Some problem that isn't the property itself, but the owners, and that makes it below the market by 20%, 30% or 50%. How to find these properties? Well, first of all, following the 100:10:3:1 rule.

Second, you should look for people who are a **#NOWANTERS**. People who for some reason no longer want the property, for them it's a costly obstacle and they just want to get rid of it. What can cause a person to be a **#NOWANTERS**? Well, there are several reasons such as divorces, fights between siblings over inheritances, moving to other cities or countries. It also happens because the person isn't very involved in the real estate market and doesn't know the market prices. On the other hand, they may not have the money to pay for property charges such as taxes or community fees and have either to sell it or lose it. They may not care because it isn't their business and they are focused on other things or moved to another country. Perhaps, they're an investor who has changed strategy and now wants to invest in other types of properties. Properties of this type are often neglected, because no one maintains them. Most likely, with a coat of paint and a few fixes here and there, you can turn it around and make it very attractive, if it is well placed. You can find these properties as long as you are willing to do 100:10:3:1. That's why when you buy a property you'll do a great deal, regardless of whether the market goes up or down in the future. If you want it as a beef cow, you will sell it in a short amount of time at market price, after having fixed it a bit. If you want it as a dairy cow, it will give you better returns on investments because you bought it at a good price versus the income you will receive.

Key 3. Location, Location, Location.

The most important thing is where the property is located. Real estate deals are about creating value for the property or the deal. You can do a lot to improve your property, but there is almost nothing you can do for the neighborhood or the building where it's located. You can reform it from head to toe, paint it, do spectacular marketing, but if the neighborhood is bad, or it's next to a noisy highway, or it has a high ratio of crime and the neighbors are undesirable, or any large BUT, you will not be able to retain tenants for a long time and the business will be very expensive and unprofitable. You can also project rents, change the use to rent by rooms or tourism, but if you have problems with regulations and laws, your plans won't matter much, you'll lose money.

You must find the worst property in the best place; the ugly duckling that can be a swan. One of the things we like most about real estate investment is the possibility of adding value to it. In the stock market, even in real estate funds type REITs (Real Estate Investment trust, they're an investment vehicle born in the United States and later moved to Europe), it doesn't depend on you but on the market that rises or decrease in value, because it's someone else who manages the property. On the other hand, in a property belonging to you, you can add value, be it cosmetic, functional or to the business as such (for example, changing it from long-term rental to tourism), making it more attractive, improving demand and also the price of the property or amount of rent you can charge.

Do your due-dilligence, not only about the city where you are going to invest, but also the neighborhood and even the block. What is the public transportation like? The parking lot? The proximity of workplaces? Is the population growing or decreasing? Have they closed production plants that gave many jobs?

What prospects are there looking forward to new job opportunities in that location? Is it located in an attractive place for students? Does your property have places like supermarkets nearby? All these factors give you information about whether if it's a good location, and that is the most important key when buying.

That's how most often people end up paying more and losing money, because of inexperience and not doing their due-dilligence thoroughly. Most of the times, your investment will be safe if it's a good location, otherwise, no matter how cheap you buy it for, you will be buying into a problem.

INFO-ENTREPRENEURSHIP: MONETIZE YOUR KNOWLEDGE

W hat can you teach us? Today influencers, YouTubers and opinion leaders are trending. The world is hungry to learn about different topics and they are looking for experts to teach them the secrets, the keys, the step by step and the procedures within the different activities; from how to fly a drone, to how to become a great entrepreneur. All this seems new, but it's not. It started a long time ago with something very simple, called "the info-product" (an information product that today you can sell online). Following the line of this book, it is about *monetizing your knowledge*. In the same way that we have talked about monetizing your consumption and your social media, now you can monetize your knowledge, talent and experience.

Info-products have been on the market for a long time. It is selling knowledge through different means. Pioneers such as Earl Nightingale (1921-1989), who was a writer and had a radio show began sharing with others different formulas for personal success and fulfillment. As technology has advanced, we have also had access to other types of tools that help share knowledge, apart from books and radio, such as audios, which began to circulate in the middle of the 20th century and went through different processes such as cassettes, audio books, mp3s, media hosting websites, etc. It's obvious that with the Internet explosion, the spread of this information has global reach and today we can share from our cell phones and for free or paying very little, small inspirational phrases, short videos on how to do something, classes, complete seminars of various days, and even extensive or technical workshops.

In addition to everything, it is an unquestionable reality that this type of learning is very much suited to today's world and what awaits us in the future. In fact, this book is being completed under the confinement imposed by the government in the midst of the Coronavirus crisis. We came to Latin America to do a tour of 11 face-to-face events, between conferences and workshops, and found out that after the first weekend everything had been canceled due to different governmental and corporate guidelines, seeking to safeguard people's health. We consciously and willingly welcomed the measures taken, understanding that it was for the good of all and understanding how health is above business. That, however, didn't change the fact that many people had bought their tickets to go and learn, and were looking forward to receiving the training workshops; nor did it change the fact that we would have a negative financial impact for expenses we had incurred due to the cancelations.

With an exemplary group of entrepreneurs, we reacted quickly and moved to the virtual world and in just 8 days we were able to carry out an event where more than 2,700 online access points were connected, which represented at least five or six thousand people learning behind their screens. We estimate that it's twice as many people as we would have had at face-to-face events. We are very happy to have been able to share keys to financial freedom at this virtual event. Keys like the ones we have shared with you in this book, which we know when applied change lives. It is our mission to help others raise their Financial IQ. We were also able to cover the expenses of the events, air tickets, etc., which was very good.

During this Coronavirus pandemic, which I'm sure will change the world and the collective consciousness of humanity, we have seen exceptional things. Yoga classes by Zoom, telecommuting on a massive level, conferences, birthday celebrations, coffee and beer hang outs through Facetime, wine drinking and snacks between friends and couples, card playing and poker with friends who used to meet up once a week and now are doing it with apps and simultaneous video calls.

In addition to the current huge and unexpected pandemic, there are many other things happening that will lead people to increasingly want to be at home and learn from there. Things like pollution and poor air quality, which increasingly create more environmental alerts in cities, strong storms and extreme temperatures caused by climate change, unbearable traffic due to city roads saturated with cars, growing insecurity, new outbreaks of different viruses and diseases, are some of the reasons that will lead us to seek the safe space of our homes to work, socialize and learn different things.

On the one hand, as you can see, your audience will be waiting for you. On the other hand, technology will continue to advance, providing us with the best tools for connectivity. 5G networks are already being implemented around the world giving greater connection speed, range, eliminating pauses, lags and screen freezes. Being able to follow people we admire on social media has made us approach mentors and have access to their latest posts, events or info-products almost instantly. In addition, virtual and augmented reality is on the rise and our brain finds it difficult to distinguish between a virtual world and a real one, making meetings, social interactions, and learning in entrepreneurship spaces increasingly attractive makink us feel closer every day. The technology already exists, like VR glasses, which allow you to live 3D experiences with your business partners, clients or family. These devices will become widespread, like everything else. Imagine being at home and sharing your knowledge with people from all over the world, because you will also be translated into any language in real time, feeling that you are with those people, seeing their body and facial expressions and using your whole body to communicate. This devices already exist and will enhance the entire info-product industry like never before.

I remember when I started doing virtual meetings, I felt like there was a barrier that separated us and that it was difficult to connect with others. It was just a matter of practice. Today, I tell the other person to get themselves a hot drink so we can have a coffee date together through WhatsApp. I put my phone in a place where the person can have a visually pleasant experience, creating an atmosphere like sitting at my dining room table, an open space or the living room of the house. I can even use a virtual background! I have people who have told me: "I feel like I'm there with you." Practice makes perfect my friend. The faster you start and the more you do it, the better you'll be at it... remember what we have already learned: "Everything worth doing is worth doing wrong until you get it right." Learning to function in the virtual world is not only worth it, but it's an imperative need in these days.

The world is ready for you to burst in with your knowledge and your info-products. What are you going to teach us? Will you give tips on Health, food, business, sports, spirituality, or investments? What will you become an expert at, if you aren't already?

Of course, I recommend that you be authentic and teach things that you yourself have learned, experienced and verified through your own experiences. That's where the real value lies, providing verified content. It doesn't count reading a couple of books and calling yourself an expert so you can go out and sell unproven philosophy. The world is already full of fake chatterboxes and we don't need more. Constantly, many of the so-called YouTubers and influencers are exposed as liars because they're not congruent and don't apply what they preach. From the one who teaches a vegan lifestyle, so that later their friends can take photos and videos of them eating meat, to the one who teaches how to get rich overnight and is broke.

Whatever you want to share and teach, make sure they're things that you have experienced in your life, because otherwise, how are you different from others? We need real mentors, influencers and opinion leaders. People are hungry for real knowledge and real leaders. As we said in another section of this book, people will check not your lips but your feet. Where have you been in recent years, what have you done, who have you helped improve their life.

I'm not telling you that you have to spend the next 20 years doing something so that later you can teach it. You may be a young person who's just starting out and you may think you have nothing to teach, so you assume that this option isn't for you. However, keep in mind that success and knowledge in an area can be achieved quickly today. We handle a magic number that we have learned: 10,000 hours. When you spend 10,000 hours learning and doing something, you become an expert. Depending on the intensity and passion with which you develop it, it will be equivalent to between 5 and 10 years. We have done well over 10,000 hours as entrepreneurs and as investors, so we can speak to you with conviction.

Ultimately, it is about being yourself and living your own life, so that later you can contribute the lessons you've learned and the keys to success in that area that you've mastered.

CONCLUSION

ASSEMBLING
THE PUZZLE

I t's time to put it all together. Like all big projects, your financial freedom and prosperity require an excellent plan that has several ingredients. First of all, you've become aware of the importance of having more money every month and how it´s fundamental for your future to have a positive cashflow. You have understood the value of money in time, the magic of compound interest, and how it's worth saving for the purpose of making investments with the capital you save. You have the keys to hack into your biology, pay yourself first, and use deferred gratification to have the emotional intelligence to be persistent and consistent with your financial plan for freedom. Also, you understand if it's better to save or pay off the debts that you find yourself having in this moment, and you can make good decisions in regards to that.

Restructuring your debts and expenses is in your hands, with attitude and without allowing anyone to pressure you. You will join the **#STOP_Financial_Bullying** campaign and never again allow others to induce you into making bad decisions with your money and becoming a financial slave. With a lot of attitude, you will restructure and budget your different monthly expenses, such as services and consumption; and you'll be a smart buyer, collecting all the current market information, promotions and the possibility of buying from manufacturers, *monetizing your consumption* and that way freeing up the micro-costs of your life so as to release cashflows and apply them to your financial plan.

At the same time, you will be able to increase your income progressively. The formula that we have exposed in this book consists of three large pillars that are part of the machinery that will take you to freedom. Those pillars are, in first place, your *traditional activity* with which you are going to be able to start up your plan without major risks, because while it takes off you will have the sustenance for you and your family. Don´t quit your job, there is no need and in the future you can do it without hazard, if that is what you want.

Second, your *low cost venture*, with which you will create your *money-making machine*, which doesn't depend 100% on your daily activity and which will create increasing cashflows. With this, initially, you will be able to clean up the past and the bad decisions you made, doing a purification of your finances; a true *financial detox*. This way, you'll be able to gradually and systematically erase your bad debts and create a powerful *freedom cashflow* that will be like a growing army under your command, with which you can also start saving, creating a financial cushion that will give you peace of mind in case of emergencies and long-term security.

Finally, *investing* is the third pillar, that'll allow you to create other assets that in turn will flood your financial buckets with security, growth, expansion and wealth.

This process, following it from beginning to end, will lead you to financial security and you won't have to worry about your survival or that of your family again, since their expenses will be covered by assets that generate cashflows. You'll then achieve financial independence, not only having your security covered, but your current lifestyle, with some pleasures and entertainment.

Then, it is up to you to jump to the next level, which is financial freedom. The formula is the same, keep creating cashflow, adding new assets and investments that add money cashflows to your life and keep growing your money-making machine. Don't settle for the only life you can get, but for the one you want, the one that you and your family deserve.

And dear reader, it doesn't have to stop there, although we know that for many it's enough. But if you are one of those dreamers who want to live life to its fullest potential and have the best experiences available, there is still a next level, which we call "absolute financial freedom". Following what is stated in this book for a long time, will allow you to reach that level. In this level, money no longer exists nor is it relevant for making your decisions. You simply go through life choosing the best of the best, the best things and the best experiences, without looking at prices and without limiting yourself in anything. It's a true life without limits. Is it for everyone? Of course not, but if you're one of those who want everything, without a doubt it's for you and we know you can achieve it.

The moment of truth has arrived and it is now when you have the opportunity to take different actions in your life. Ultimately, what we want is that, to go out and act differently so we can harvest different results. However, all action is preconceived by a decision. When we were new to entrepreneurship, we heard a phrase that marked us: "in life you can have a million dollars or a million excuses, but not both." We can validate the reality of this phrase after our trajectory. Those who say vs. those who do, those who help vs. those who ask for help, those who are part of the solution or are part of the problem, the victim or the person responsible. You decide on which side of the equation you are going to stand on. Especially in these times, now more than ever, we need responsible people to help light the way and empower others.

We know that ultimately what happens in your life and the application of the knowledge in this book will depend on an emotional decision. As we have stated before, human beings only move in life to avoid pain and/or seek pleasure. Faced with a situation as extreme as that experienced in 2020, in which we have seen our way of life and even our survival threatened, it's normal for many to make a reflective and deep analysis about the lifestyle they lead until now and their financial practices. More than ever, it is becoming clear that applying the principles of financial intelligence that we share in this book must be priority. We hope that there'll be a new rebirth of consciousness in most people and in your own life, because we know that this way, what you have learned in these pages will have a positive and profound impact on your life.

We thank you for reaching the end of this book and for allowing us to share our knowledge and experiences with you. It is exciting to receive messages of gratitude through our social media accounts, from people who have attended our workshops or have received advice. It's awesome the stories like "after the financial intelligence workshop we immediately started saving $200 a month", "we started saving for the first time and we already have a financial cushion that allows us to sleep peacefully", "we've bought our first property that is generating us an income "," we decided to start up a business and today we have our money-making machine that produces us so much per month ","" we have put your advice into practice and today we have financial freedom." We are excited to know that our contributions, based on our experience, have been useful to others who have also applied and improved their lives.

We ask you then, that if what you have learned here made a positive impact on your life, you write us a message through our social media accounts telling us your experience, how this book helped you and how you were able to turn your life around achieving better results.

Thanks to what we learned and shared with you in this book, we were able to fix our financial situations and have been prospering for quite some time now. We are so grateful that others before us were willing to share this valuable information that is life-transforming. Reaching financial freedom is a great achievement that has a positive impact on all areas of your life. Today, however, what makes us happiest is knowing that our experience helps others and thus we feel that we have a purpose in our life. We have been able to transcend, leaving a legacy by adding value to the lives of others. That's true prosperity and abundance, when your own experience overflows for the benefit of others. We sincerely wish you that kind of wealth.

ABOUT THE AUTHOR

Cata And Fer Palacio

Cata & Fer Palacio are entrepreneurs and investors with over 20 years of experience. They have impacted hundreds of thousands of lives with their conferences, workshops and best seller "Detox Financiero". Their purpose is to raise the financial IQ of humanity and help people live better lives.

Nuestras redes sociales:

@coach_financiero
@ferycatapalacio

/coachFinancieroGlobal
/ferycatapalacio

Coach Financiero

www.coachfinanciero.net

Made in the USA
Las Vegas, NV
16 February 2025

18241060R00111